Christmas in the Country

Holiday Quilts with Farmhouse Flair

RHONDA McCRAY
OF FARMHOUSE THREADS

Martingale
Create with Confidence

Christmas in the Country:
Holiday Quilts with Farmhouse Flair

Martingale®
19021 120th Ave. NE, Ste. 102
Bothell, WA 98011-9511 USA
ShopMartingale.com

Printed in Hong Kong
25 24 23 22 21 20 8 7 6 5 4 3 2 1

Library of Congress Cataloging-in-Publication Data is available upon request.

ISBN: 978-1-68356-063-0

MISSION STATEMENT

We empower makers who use fabric and yarn to make life more enjoyable.

CREDITS

PUBLISHER AND CHIEF VISIONARY OFFICER
Jennifer Erbe Keltner

CONTENT DIRECTOR
Karen Costello Soltys

MANAGING EDITOR
Tina Cook

ACQUISITIONS AND DEVELOPMENT EDITOR
Laurie Baker

COPY EDITOR
Sheila Chapman Ryan

DESIGN MANAGER
Adrienne Smitke

PRODUCTION MANAGER
Regina Girard

COVER DESIGNER
Kathy Kotomaimoce

BOOK DESIGNER
Angie Haupert Hoogensen

LOCATION PHOTOGRAPHER
Adam Albright

STUDIO PHOTOGRAPHER
Brent Kane

ILLUSTRATOR
Lisa Lauch

SPECIAL THANKS
Photography for this book was taken at the home of Libby Warnken of Ankeny, Iowa; and at the Garden Barn, Indianola, Iowa.

contents

introduction

Come celebrate Christmas with me! It's my favorite time of the year, and I love to create things to decorate every nook and cranny of my home until it's filled to the brim with the spirit of the holidays. Tucked within these pages are more than a dozen projects that I've made to deck my own living space for the season and to give as gifts.

There never seems to be enough time to get everything done, and the clock spins especially fast during the holidays. There's so much to do! But as much as I love shopping for each special gift, making cookies and Christmas crafts with the grandkids, and preparing the holiday meal, I also try to make time for a little stitching each day. Putting needle and thread to fabric helps me relax—and before I know it, I have a finished project.

Perfect for busy stitchers, most of these projects can be put together relatively quickly. Start with the Christmas Bowl Fillers (page 61) and make one each night. By the end of the week, you'll find that your bowl is full and you've had time to make a couple Mistletoe Ornaments (page 73) as well! Table runners and candle mats are also great to make when you don't have lots of time, and they're great gifts. Cut out all your pieces one night, assembly line sew them together the next, and before you know it, you'll have several more gifts finished and taking their place under the tree.

If you love snowmen as much as I do, you'll enjoy plenty of designs that incorporate these cool characters. Snow is rare in Southern California where I live, so the only way for me to build a snowman is to do it from fabric. From the littlest flakes found in the borders of the Tree-Trimming Party Quilt (page 41) to the long-on-cheer Slim the Snowman Runner (page 33), each snowman brings his own unique personality to the party. Many of the projects can be left on display beyond the holidays—they're perfect for brightening a winter day!

Christmas fills my heart with so many good feelings, and making handmade items is part of that joy. Whether you make just one project or many, I hope that you, too, find pleasure in all that the season has to offer. Happy holidays!

~ Rhonda

Oh the weather outside is frightful
but the fire is so delightful
and since theres no place to go.
Let it Snow · Let it Snow · Let it Snow

let it snow quilt

Whether or not you have a white Christmas, these adorable snowmen are hard to resist. The easy-to-make Snowball blocks quickly become faces with a bit of fusible appliqué and an assortment of decorative buttons and snaps.

materials

Yardage is based on 42"-wide fabric. Fat eighths measure 9" × 21".

8 fat eighths of assorted prints for block corners and outer border

⅝ yard of mottled tan print or tea-dyed muslin for blocks and inner border

⅔ yard of green print for outer border and binding

4" × 4½" rectangle of orange felted wool for noses

2" × 3" rectangle of black felted wool for eyes and mouth

1 yard of fabric for backing

32" × 38" piece of batting

7" square of lightweight paper-backed fusible web

6-strand embroidery floss in orange and black

Size 7 embroidery needle

16 assorted black buttons, ⅜" to ⅝" diameter, for eyes

6 assorted black buttons, ¼" diameter, for mouth

12 black snap sets, ¼" diameter, for mouths

Glad Press'n Seal plastic wrap (optional)

cutting

All measurements include ¼"-wide seam allowances.

From the assorted prints, cut a *total* of:

- 20 squares, 4" × 4"; cut into quarters diagonally to yield 80 triangles
- 48 squares, 2" × 2"

From the tan print, cut:

- 2 strips, 6½" × 42"; crosscut into 12 squares, 6½" × 6½"
- 2 strips, 2" × 28"
- 2 strips, 2¼" × 18½"

From the green print, cut:

- 5 strips, 2¼" × 42"; crosscut into 80 squares, 2¼" × 2¼". Cut each square in half diagonally to yield 160 triangles.
- 4 strips, 2½" × 42"

making the blocks

Use a ¼" seam allowance. Press the seam allowances as indicated by the arrows.

1 Draw a diagonal line from corner to corner on the wrong side of each assorted 2" square.

2 Place a marked square on each corner of a tan 6½" square, right sides together. Sew on the marked lines. Trim ¼" from the stitching lines. Press. The block should measure 6½" square, including seam allowances. Repeat to make a total of 12 blocks.

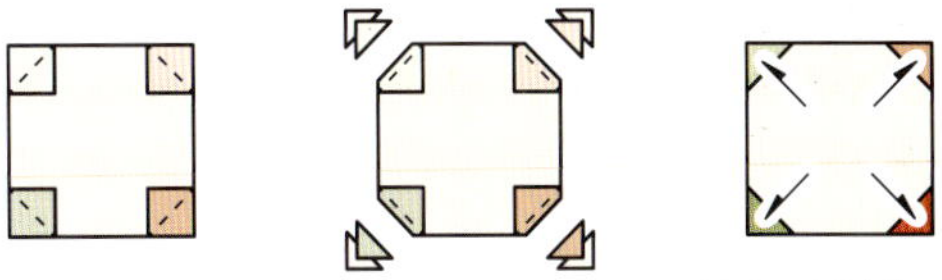

Make 12 blocks, 6½" × 6½".

FINISHED QUILT
27½" × 33½"

FINISHED BLOCK
6" × 6"

assembling the quilt top

1 Refer to the assembly diagram to arrange the blocks in four horizontal rows of three blocks each. Sew the blocks in each row together. Press. Join the rows. Press. The quilt center should measure 18½" × 24½", including seam allowances.

Quilt-center assembly

2 Sew the tan 2¼" × 18½" inner-border strips to the top and bottom edges of the quilt top. Press. Join the tan 2" × 28" inner-border strips to the sides of the quilt top. Press. The quilt top should measure 22" × 28", including seam allowances.

3 To make the outer border, sew a green triangle to one diagonal edge of a print triangle. Press. Repeat on the opposite diagonal edge to make a flying-geese unit. Press. Repeat to make a total of 80 units measuring 1⅞" × 3¼", including seam allowances.

Make 80
flying-geese units,
1⅞" × 3¼".

4 Join 20 flying-geese units as shown to make an A strip. Press. Repeat to make a total of two A strips measuring 3¼" × 28", including seam allowances.

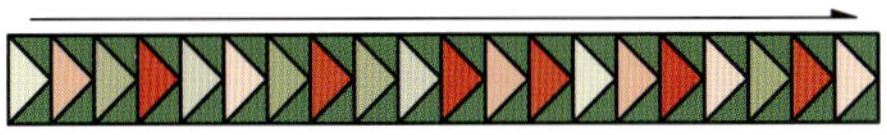

Make 2 A strips,
3¼" × 28".

5 Join 18 flying-geese units in a horizontal row as shown. Press. Repeat to make a total of two strips. Join the remaining flying-geese units into two pairs. Press. Sew a pair to the left end of each strip to complete the B strips. Each strip should measure 3¼" × 28", including seam allowances.

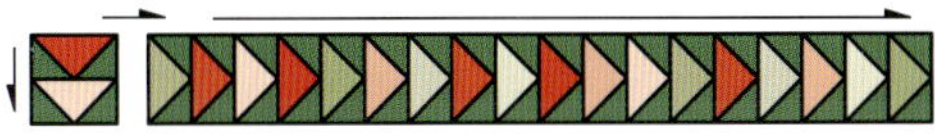

Make 2 B strips,
3¼" × 28".

6 Referring to the diagram for the proper orientation, sew the A strips to the sides of the quilt top. Press. Join the B strips to the top and bottom edges of the quilt top. Press. The quilt top should measure 27½" × 33½".

Adding borders

7 Referring to the photo on page 8 for placement, transfer the verse on pullout pattern sheet 1 onto the inner border. Using three strands of black floss, backstitch the letters and make a French knot for each dot.

Glad Press'n Seal transfer method

To easily transfer the lettering onto the inner border, trace the words for one side of the quilt onto the smooth side of a piece of Press'n Seal plastic wrap. With the sticky side down, position the marked piece of Press'n Seal on the appropriate border strip and smooth it into place. Embroider the words. Remove the Press'n Seal by making cuts in the plastic wrap and gently tearing it away from the fabric. Use tweezers to remove any small pieces that may be left under the embroidery. Repeat the process for the remaining three borders.

finishing the quilt

If you need detailed instructions about any of the finishing steps, download free information at ShopMartingale.com/HowtoQuilt.

1. Layer the backing, batting, and quilt top. Baste the layers together.

2. Quilt by hand or machine. The quilt shown is machine quilted with an overall meandering pattern.

3. Using the green 2½"-wide strips, make the binding and attach it to the quilt.

4. Using the patterns on pullout pattern sheet 1 and referring to "Fusible-Web Appliqué" on page 78, prepare 12 noses and 13 circles for eyes and mouths.

5. Refer to the appliqué placement guide at right to fuse the appliqués in place. With two strands of matching floss and the embroidery needle, whipstitch the appliqués in place. Separate the snap sets into male and female halves; discard or set aside the female halves for another project. Stitch the male snap halves and the buttons to the blocks for the eyes and mouths using two strands of black floss.

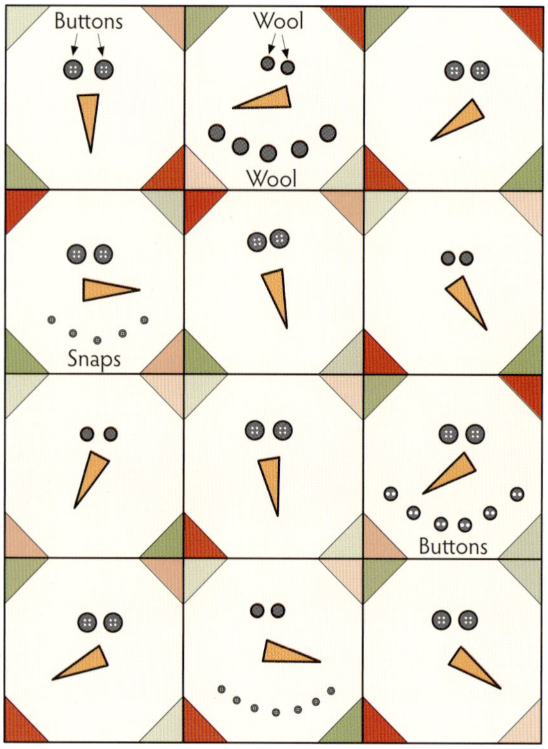

Appliqué placement guide

white christmas quilt

For some, it doesn't quite feel like the holidays without at least a sprinkling of snow. Whether there's a possibility of flakes or not, this sentimental wall hanging will let everyone know what you're wishing for.

materials

Yardage is based on 42"-wide fabric.

⅔ yard of charcoal solid for background

17" × 20" rectangle of off-white felted wool for letters, appliquéd snowflake, and snow

5" × 10" rectangle of red felted wool for upper banner and holly berries

3" × 11" rectangle of sage felted wool for lower banner

6" × 11" rectangle of dark green felted wool for holly leaves

Scraps of assorted green felted wools for trees

2" × 6" rectangle of brown wool for tree trunks

⅝ yard of green print for inner border and binding

⅝ yard of red stripe for borders

1 yard of fabric for backing

33" × 42" piece of batting

#12 pearl cotton in colors to match wools

#8 pearl cotton in off-white

Size 24 chenille needle

Size 7 embroidery needle

Lightweight paper-backed fusible web

White fine-tip pen for transferring embroidery designs (I used a Sakura Gelly Roll pen) or Glad Press'n Seal plastic wrap

cutting

All measurements include ¼"-wide seam allowances.

From the charcoal solid, cut:

- 1 rectangle, 20" × 29"

From the green print, cut:

- 3 strips, 1⅞" × 42"; crosscut into 47 squares, 1⅞" × 1⅞"
- 4 strips, 2½" × 42"

From the red stripe, cut:

- 3 strips, 1⅞" × 42"; crosscut into 47 squares, 1⅞" × 1⅞"
- 3 strips, 3½" × 42"; crosscut into:
    - 2 strips, 3½" × 35½"
    - 2 strips, 3½" × 20½"

I'm
Dreaming
of a
WHITE
CHRISTMAS
JUST LIKE THE
ONES I USED TO
KNOW

appliquéing the design

Refer to "Fusible-Web Appliqué" on page 78 and "Embroidery Stitches" on page 79 for complete information on preparing the appliqués and fusing and stitching them in place.

1 Using the patterns on pullout pattern sheet 2, prepare the appliqués. The patterns for the holly leaves and berries are on pattern sheet 1.

2 Refer to the pattern and the photo on page 14 to fuse all of the shapes except for the holly leaves and berries to the charcoal rectangle, centering the design on the rectangle.

3 Using one strand of off-white #12 pearl cotton and the embroidery needle, whipstitch the letters to the background and banners. Blanket-stitch around each banner and the remaining wool shapes using matching #12 pearl cotton.

4 Backstitch the detail lines on the upper banner with one strand of red #12 pearl cotton.

embroidering the design

The embroidery designs are given on pullout pattern sheet 2 to guide you in positioning the appliqués. The snowflakes and the lines above and below *WHITE CHRISTMAS* can be traced as is from the complete design, but because the design is shown in reverse for fusible appliqué, refer to the photo on page 14 to position the embroidery elements. The words *JUST LIKE THE* are given separately on the pattern sheet as they should be traced.

1 Use a light box or window and the white marking pen to transfer the embroidery designs onto the appliquéd charcoal rectangle (or use the Glad Press'n Seal method on page 9 to trace the embroidery designs onto the plastic wrap and adhere each motif to the charcoal rectangle). Refer to the photo as needed for placement. If you have trouble seeing the designs through the dark fabric, trace over the lines on the pattern with a black marker to make them more visible.

2 Using one strand of off-white #8 pearl cotton and the chenille needle, stitch the embroidery designs as follows. Refer to "Embroidery Stitches" as needed.

- Backstitch the lines of each snowflake and make a French knot where indicated by a dot.
- Stem-stitch the solid lines and backstitch the dashed lines above and below the words *WHITE CHRISTMAS.*
- Backstitch the words *JUST LIKE THE.*

3 If you've used plastic wrap, remove it now. Keeping the design centered, trim the appliquéd and embroidered rectangle to 18½" × 27½".

adding the borders

Use a ¼" seam allowance. Press the seam allowances as indicated by the arrows.

1 Draw a diagonal line from corner to corner on the wrong side of each red 1⅞" square. Layer a marked square on top of a green 1⅞" square, right sides together. Sew ¼" from both sides of the marked line. Cut the squares apart on the marked line to make two half-square-triangle units. Press. Repeat to make a total of 94 units measuring 1½" square, including seam allowances.

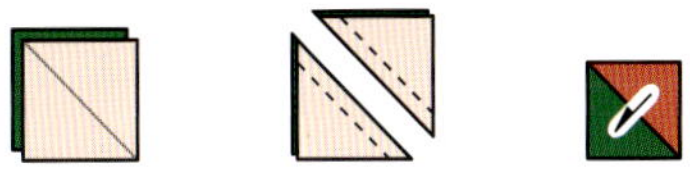

Make 94 units, 1½" × 1½".

2 Join 18 half-square-triangle units as shown to make an A strip. Press. Repeat to make a total of two A strips measuring 1½" × 18½", including seam allowances.

Make 2 A strips, 1½" × 18½".

FINISHED QUILT
26½" × 35½"

3 Join 29 half-square-triangle units as shown to make a B strip. Press. The strip should measure 1½" × 29½", including seam allowances.

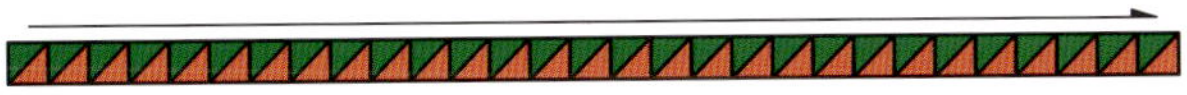

Make 1 B strip, 1½" × 29½".

4 Repeat step 3 with the remaining 29 half-square-triangle units to make a C strip as shown.

Make 1 C strip, 1½" × 29½".

5 Referring to the quilt assembly diagram below for the proper orientation, sew the A strips to the top and bottom edges of the appliquéd quilt top. Press. Join the B strip to the right edge of the quilt top and the C strip to the left edge. Press. The quilt top should measure 20½" × 29½", including seam allowances.

6 Sew the red 3½" × 20½" strips to the top and bottom edges of the quilt top. Press. Join the red 3½" × 35½" strips to the sides of the quilt top. The quilt top should now measure 26½" × 35½".

Quilt assembly

7 Refer to the photo to fuse three holly berries and three leaves to each corner of the outer border. Using one strand of matching #12 pearl cotton and the embroidery needle, whipstitch the berries in place and blanket-stitch around each leaf.

finishing the quilt

If you need detailed instructions about any of the finishing steps, download free information at ShopMartingale.com/HowtoQuilt.

1 Layer the backing, batting, and quilt top. Baste the layers together.

2 If desired, quilt by hand or machine. While the wall hanging shown is not quilted, you can quilt in the ditch around the borders for stability and around each appliqué shape to make the design stand out.

3 Using the green 2½"-wide strips, make the binding and attach it to the quilt.

1
2
3
4
5
6
7
8
9
10
11
12
13
14
15
16
17
18
19
20
21
22
23
24
25

advent tree quilt

Count down the days leading up to Christmas with little goody-filled stockings.

materials

Yardage is based on 42"-wide fabric.

1⅜ yards of mottled tan print or tea-dyed muslin for background and outer border

⅓ yard *total* of assorted red prints for inner border

⅛ yard of brown print for tree trunk

¼ yard *total* of assorted green prints for tree limbs

7" × 7" square of red print #1 for star

⅜ yard of red print #2 for binding

1½ yards of fabric for backing

34" × 52" piece of batting

25 rectangles, 2½" × 5" *each,* of assorted felted wools in reds, greens, golds, and tans for stocking fronts

¼ yard of black felted wool for stocking backs

#8 pearl cotton in black

Size 24 chenille needle

25 assorted buttons, ¾" to 1" diameter, for stocking hangers

25 key tags, 1¼" diameter, for dates

Number stamp set, ½", and red stamp pad for dates*

Strong-brewed coffee

Water-soluble fabric marker

**You could use a permanent red marker to write the numbers instead.*

cutting

All measurements include ¼"-wide seam allowances.

From the tan print, cut:

- 1 strip, 6½" × 42"; crosscut into:
  - 2 rectangles, 6½" × 10½"
  - 1 rectangle, 4½" × 10½"
- 4 strips, 4½" × 42"; crosscut into:
  - 1 rectangle, 4½" × 21½"
  - 9 rectangles, 4½" × 10½"
- 1 strip, 3½" × 42"; crosscut into 2 rectangles, 3½" × 10½"
- 11 strips, 1½" × 42"; crosscut *8* of the strips into:
  - 2 strips, 1½" × 27½"
  - 2 rectangles, 1½" × 6½"
  - 2 rectangles, 1½" × 5½"
  - 2 rectangles, 1½" × 4½"
  - 2 rectangles, 1½" × 3½"
  - 2 rectangles, 1½" × 2½"
  - 130 squares, 1½" × 1½"

Continued on page 18

Continued from page 17

From the brown print, cut:

- 2 strips, 1½" × 42"; crosscut into:
  - 1 rectangle, 1½" × 6½"
  - 5 rectangles, 1½" × 4½"
  - 1 rectangle, 1½" × 3½"
  - 6 squares, 1½" × 1½"

From the assorted green prints, cut a *total* of:

- 78 squares, 1½" × 1½"

From the assorted red prints, cut a *total* of:

- 128 squares, 1½" × 1½"

From red print #2, cut:

- 4 strips, 2½" × 42"

assembling the quilt top

Use a ¼" seam allowance. Press the seam allowances of each row in one direction, alternating the direction from row to row.

1 To make the tree-trunk units, sew a tan 3½" × 10½" rectangle to each long edge of a brown 1½" × 3½" rectangle. Press. The unit should measure 3½" × 21½", including seam allowances. In the same manner, sew a tan 4½" × 10½" rectangle to each long edge of a brown 1½" × 4½" rectangle. Press. Repeat to make a total of five units measuring 4½" × 21½", including seam allowances. Finally, sew a tan 6½" × 10½" rectangle to each long edge of a brown 1½" × 6½" rectangle to make one unit measuring 6½" × 21½".

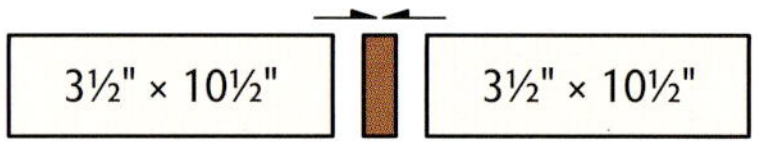

Make 1 unit, 3½" × 21½".

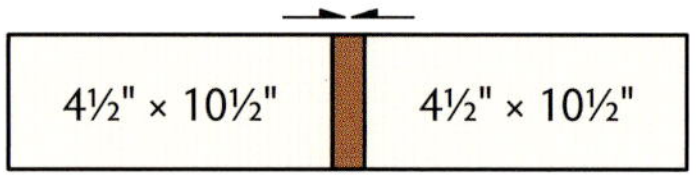

Make 5 units, 4½" × 21½".

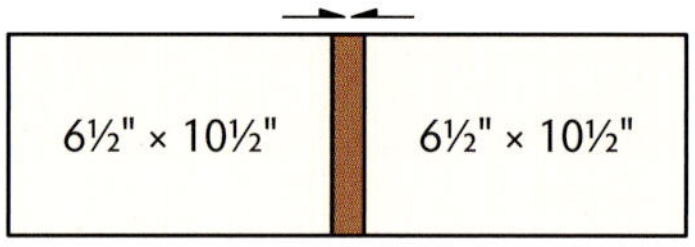

Make 1 unit, 6½" × 21½".

2 To make tree-branch units, sew the remaining tan rectangles, two tan 1½" squares, the assorted green 1½" squares, and the brown 1½" squares in horizontal rows as shown. Press. Each row should measure 1½" × 21½", including seam allowances.

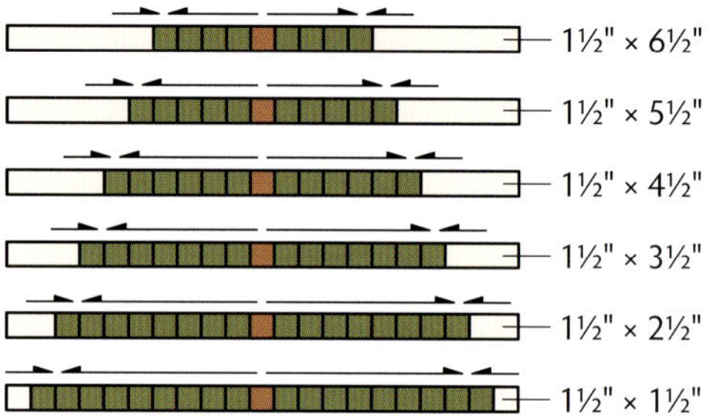

Make 1 of each unit, 1½" × 21½".

3 Refer to the quilt-center assembly diagram to arrange the trunk and branch units in 13 horizontal rows as shown. Join the rows. Press. Sew the tan 4½" × 21½" rectangle to the top of the tree unit. Press. The quilt center should measure 21½" × 39½", including seam allowances.

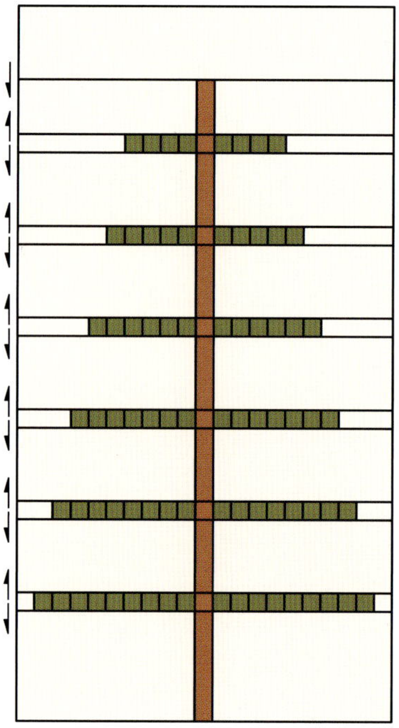

Quilt-center assembly

FINISHED QUILT
27½" × 45½"

4 Sew each of the remaining tan 1½" squares to a red 1½" square. Press. Make 128 units measuring 1½" × 2½", including seam allowances.

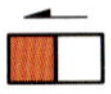

Make 128 units, 1½" × 2½".

5 Join 39 units from step 4 along the long edges to make a row, alternating the colors. Press. The row should measure 2½" × 39½", including seam allowances. Repeat to make a total of two side borders. In the same manner, join 25 units from step 4 to make the top border measuring 2½" × 25½", including seam allowances. Repeat to make the bottom border.

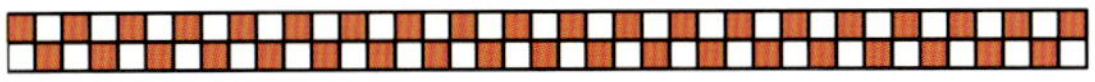

Make 2 side borders, 2½" × 39½".

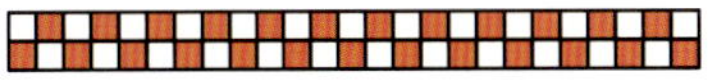

Make 2 top/bottom borders, 2½" × 25½".

6 Refer to the quilt assembly diagram on page 20 to sew the side borders to the sides of the quilt top. Press. Join the top and bottom borders to the quilt top. The quilt top should measure 25½" × 43½", including seam allowances.

7 Join the remaining tan 1½" × 42" strips end to end to make one long strip. Press. From the pieced strip, cut two strips, 1½" × 43½". Sew these strips to the sides of the quilt top. Press. Join the tan 1½" × 27½" strips to the top and bottom of the quilt top. Press. The quilt top should measure 27½" × 45½".

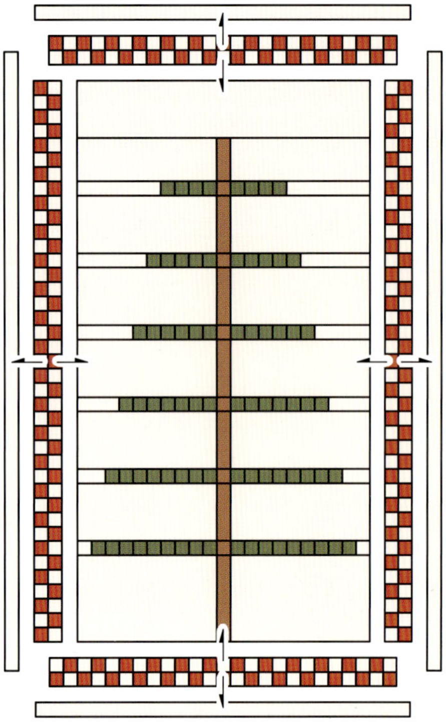

Quilt assembly

8 Using the pattern on pullout pattern sheet 1, cut one star from the red print #1 square and use your favorite turned-edge appliqué method to stitch it to the top of the tree trunk with matching thread.

finishing the quilt

If you need detailed instructions about any of the finishing steps, download free information at ShopMartingale.com/HowtoQuilt.

1 Layer the backing, batting, and quilt top. Baste the layers together.

2 Quilt by hand or machine. The quilt shown is quilted with an overall meandering pattern.

3 Using the 2½"-wide red print #2 strips, make the binding and attach it to the quilt.

making the stocking ornaments

1 To "age" the key tags, dip each one into a cup of strong-brewed coffee until it's the desired darkness; let dry.

2 Using the pattern on pullout pattern sheet 1, cut 25 stocking fronts from assorted wool rectangles and 25 stocking backs from the black wool.

3 With the black pearl cotton and the chenille needle, sew a key tag to each stocking front, ½" from the upper edge.

4 Pin a stocking front to a stocking back, wrong sides together. Starting at the upper-right corner and using the black pearl cotton and the chenille needle, blanket-stitch the stocking edges together. On the top edge, stitch across the front edge only, leaving the top open. When you reach the starting point, make a 1"-long hanging loop and secure the thread. Repeat to make a total of 25 stockings.

5 Lay out the stockings on the quilt top, placing them where desired along the tree branches. Use the fabric marker to mark the spot for each button. Use the pearl cotton to sew a button to each mark.

6 Stamp or hand write the numbers 1–25 on the key tags, keeping them in numerical order from top to bottom and left to right. Place a piece of sturdy cardboard under the tag to create a more stable surface when stamping or writing the numbers. Hang the stockings on the buttons.

7 Fill the stockings with tiny treats!

holiday snow runner

The perfect backdrop for this old-fashioned Christmas scene is purchased toweling. It's easy to customize to any length you need, and the long edges are already hemmed!

materials

Yardage is based on 42"-wide fabric unless otherwise indicated.

1 yard of 16"-wide khaki with red side stripes toweling for background

15" × 25" rectangle of off-white wool for houses, snowflakes, and scalloped borders

2" × 8" rectangle of pale yellow wool for windows

3" × 14" strip of red wool for doors, chimneys, and holly berries

4" × 6" rectangle of light green wool for A trees and holly leaves

6" × 8" rectangle of dark green wool for B trees

7" × 7" square of green plaid wool for C trees

2" × 3" rectangle of brown wool for tree trunks

2½" × 6" rectangle of black wool for roofs

⅝ yard of fabric for backing

¼ yard of 18"-wide Lite Steam-a-Seam 2 double-stick fusible web for scalloped borders

Lightweight paper-backed fusible web for appliqués

#12 pearl cotton in colors to match wools

Size 7 embroidery needle

Freezer paper

Water-soluble fabric marker

Basting glue (optional)

appliquéing the runner pieces

1 Referring to "Fusible-Web Appliqué" on page 78, trace the border pattern on pullout pattern sheet 1 twice onto the double-stick fusible web. Prepare two border pieces from the off-white wool.

2 Trace two additional border pieces onto the dull side of a piece of freezer paper. Roughly cut around each piece. With the shiny side against the wrong side of the off-white wool, use a dry iron to press the freezer-paper pieces in place. Cut out each piece on the marked lines. Remove the freezer paper. You'll have two borders prepared with fusible and two without.

3 Using the patterns on pullout pattern sheet 1, prepare the remaining appliqué shapes using fusible web.

4 Square up the ends of the toweling so it measures 35" long. Using the fabric marker, draw a line 1" from and parallel to each end.

5 Refer to the placement guides to position the house, tree, and snowflake appliqués on each end of the toweling, randomly placing half the G, H, and I snowflakes on each end. Position the holly leaves and berries on the two border pieces *without* fusible web. Referring to "Embroidery Stitches" on page 79 and using one strand of matching pearl cotton and the embroidery needle, whipstitch around each shape.

Runner appliqué placement guide

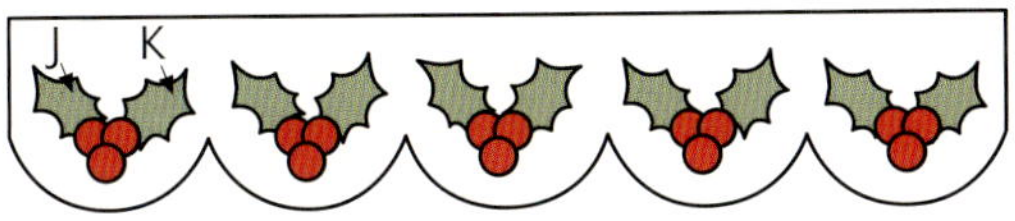

Border appliqué placement guide

6 With black pearl cotton, backstitch through the horizontal and vertical centers of each window, and then backstitch around each window.

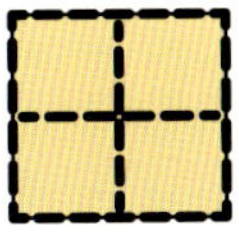

finishing the runner

1 Trim ½" from each end of the runner. Place the runner on your work surface wrong side up.

2 Remove the paper backing from the border pieces that haven't been appliquéd. Position a border piece, sticky side down, on the wrong side of one end of the runner, positioning the border straight edge ½" from the runner end and aligning the sides. The top of the border should be flush with the bottom of the house and tree appliqués. Finger-press the border in place. Repeat on the opposite end of the runner.

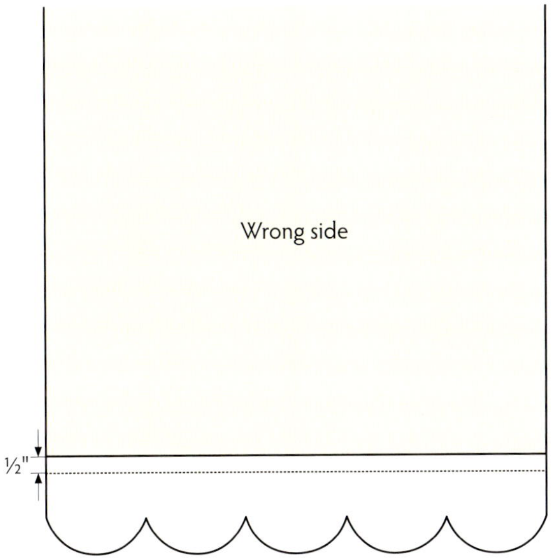

FINISHED RUNNER
16" × 39"

3 Turn the runner right side up. Position an appliquéd border piece over the sticky side of each nonappliquéd border piece, aligning the edges. Follow the manufacturer's instructions to fuse the pieces together. Using basting glue or pins, secure the front upper edge to the runner. With one strand of off-white pearl cotton, blanket-stitch around the edges of the border, stitching across the straight edges on both sides of the border.

Success with Fusibles

Not all fusible webs are created equal. Make sure you choose a lightweight fusible web so that you'll be able to stitch through the fabric without gumming up your needle. Follow the manufacturer's instructions and ensure that the appliqués have bonded to the background fabric before you permanently stitch them in place on the runner.

4 Measure the width of the runner on the back from the inside edge of the hem to the opposite inside edge of the hem. Measure the length of the runner between the straight edges of the scalloped borders. Cut a piece of backing fabric 1" wider and longer than these measurements. Press under ½" on each side of the backing piece. Slip-stitch the backing to the runner.

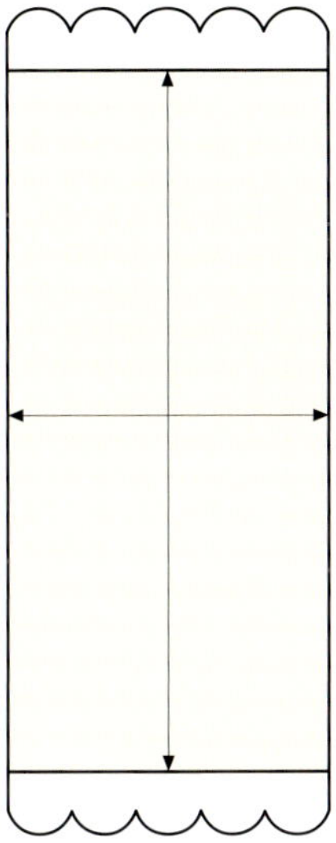

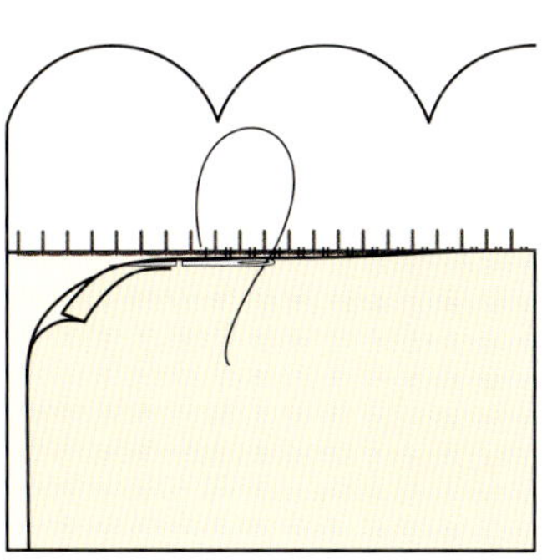

SHINY BRITE

christmas place mats

Ready to perk up your table for the holidays? These festive place mats are just the ticket!

materials for 4 place mats

Yardage is based on 42"-wide fabric.

1⅛ yards of beige print for backgrounds

¼ yard *each* of 4 assorted green prints for tree branches

⅛ yard of brown print for tree trunks

⅝ yard of red print #1 for stockings and binding

⅛ yard of red print #2 for stockings

¼ yard of cream print for stockings

¼ yard of gold print for stockings and stars

1⅜ yards of fabric for backings

1⅓ yards of batting

cutting

All measurements include ¼"-wide seam allowances.

From the beige print, cut:

- 2 strips, 6½" × 42"; crosscut into 4 pieces, 6½" × 12½"
- 1 strip, 5½" × 42"; crosscut into 4 pieces, 5½" × 8"
- 11 strips, 1½" × 42"; crosscut into:
    - 16 pieces, 1½" × 6" (A and L)
    - 8 pieces, 1½" × 5½" (B)
    - 8 pieces, 1½" × 5" (C)
    - 8 pieces, 1½" × 4½" (D)
    - 8 pieces, 1½" × 4" (E)
    - 8 pieces, 1½" × 3½" (F)
    - 8 pieces, 1½" × 3" (G)
    - 8 pieces, 1½" × 2½" (H)
    - 8 pieces, 1½" × 2" (I)
    - 8 squares, 1½" × 1½" (J)
    - 8 pieces, 1" × 1½" (K)

From *each* of the assorted green prints, cut:

- 4 strips, 1½" × 42" (16 total); randomly crosscut the strips into a *total* of:
    - 8 pieces, 1½" × 8"
    - 4 squares, 1½" × 1½" (M)
    - 4 pieces, 1½" × 2½" (N)
    - 4 pieces, 1½" × 3½" (O)
    - 4 pieces, 1½" × 4½" (P)
    - 4 pieces, 1½" × 5½" (Q)
    - 4 pieces, 1½" × 6½" (R)
    - 4 pieces, 1½" × 7½" (S)
    - 4 pieces, 1½" × 8½" (T)
    - 4 pieces, 1½" × 9½" (U)
    - 4 pieces, 1½" × 10½" (V)
    - 4 pieces, 1½" × 11½" (W)

From the brown print, cut:

- 4 squares, 1½" × 1½" (X)

From red print #1, cut:

- 1 strip, 1½" × 42"; crosscut into 4 pieces, 1½" × 8"
- 8 strips, 2" × 42"

From red print #2, cut:

- 1 strip, 1½" × 42"; crosscut into 4 pieces, 1½" × 8"

From the cream print, cut:

- 1 strip, 2" × 42"; crosscut into 4 pieces, 2" × 5½"
- 1 strip, 1½" × 42"; crosscut into 4 pieces, 1½" × 8"

From the gold print, cut:

- 1 strip, 1½" × 42"; crosscut into 4 pieces, 1½" × 8"
- 1 strip, 4" × 42"; crosscut into 8 squares, 4" × 4"

From the backing fabric, cut:

- 4 pieces, 17" × 23"

From the batting, cut:

- 4 pieces, 17" × 23"

making the place-mat tops

Use a ¼" seam allowance. Press the seam allowances as indicated by the arrows.

1 Arrange the A–X pieces in 12 rows as shown. Sew the pieces in each row together. Press. Join the rows. Press. Repeat to make a total of four blocks measuring 12½" square, including seam allowances.

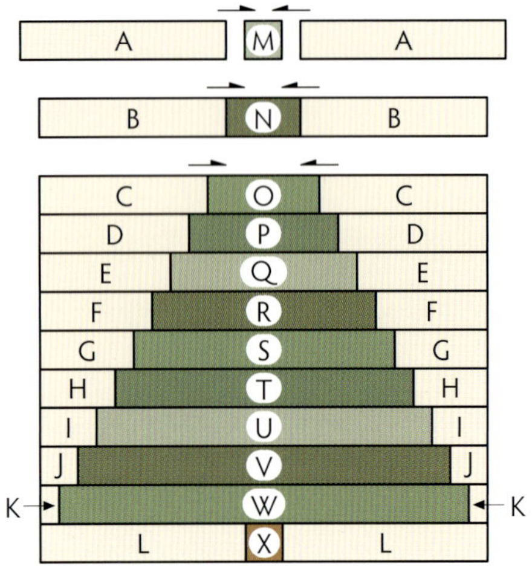

Make 4 blocks,
12½" × 12½".

2 Sew a 6½" × 12½" beige piece to the right edge of a block. Press. Repeat to make a total of four tops measuring 18½" × 12½", including seam allowances.

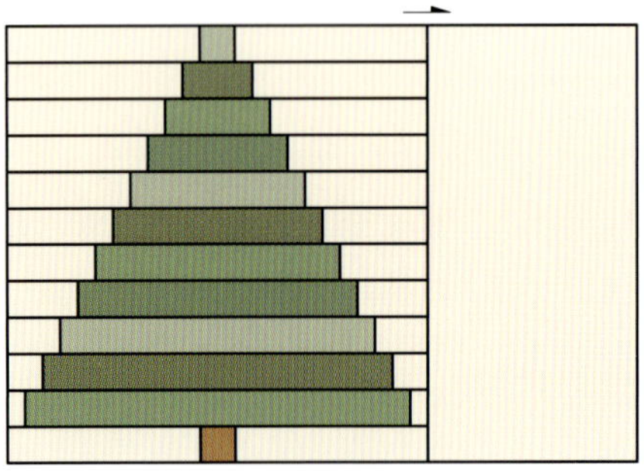

Make 4 tops,
18½" × 12½".

making the stockings and stars

1 To make the stockings, randomly sew six 1½" × 8" pieces (two green and one each of cream, gold, red #1, and red #2) together along the long edges to make a strip set. Press. Repeat to make a total of four strip sets. Crosscut each strip set into five segments, 1½" wide (20 total).

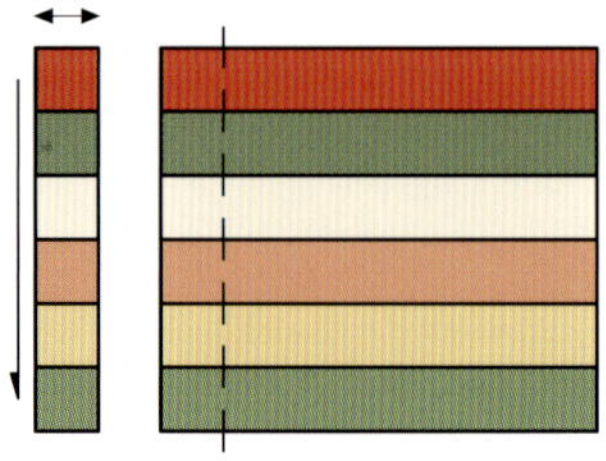

Make 4 strip sets, 6½" × 8".
Cut each strip set into
5 segments (20 total), 1½" × 6½".

2 Randomly sew five strip-set segments together along the long edges, alternating their directions to make a patchwork rectangle. Re-press seam allowances as needed so they oppose each other. Press. Repeat to make a total of four units measuring 5½" × 6½", including seam allowances. Sew a 2" × 5½" cream piece to the top of each unit. Each unit should now measure 5½" × 8", including seam allowances.

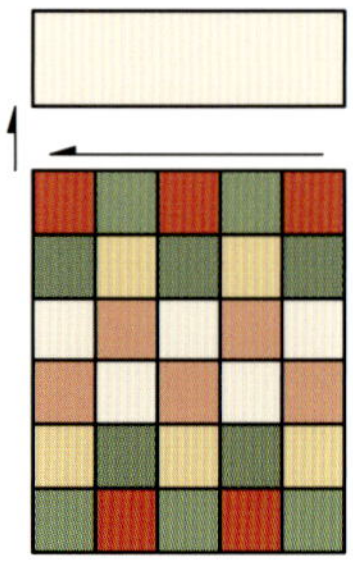

Make 4 units,
5½" × 8".

FINISHED PLACE MAT
18½" × 12½"
FINISHED BLOCK
12" × 12"

3 Trace the stocking pattern on page 31 onto the wrong side of each 5½" × 8" beige print piece, placing the top edge of the stocking ¼" from the top of the rectangle.

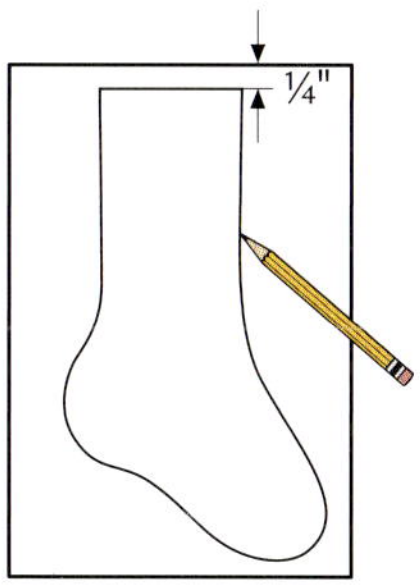

4 Layer a marked rectangle right sides together with a pieced unit from step 2. Sew on the traced line all the way around the stocking. Trim ¼" from the stitching line. Clip the curves. Cut a 2" slit in the center of the beige fabric *only*. Turn the stocking right side out through the slit. Push out the curves

and smooth the seams. Press the stocking flat. Whipstitch the slit closed. Repeat to make a total of four stockings.

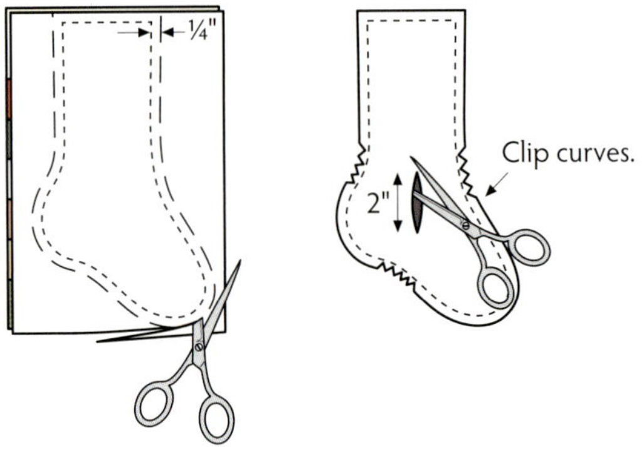

Make 4.

5 To make the stars, trace the star pattern on page 31 onto the wrong side of four gold 4" squares. Layer each marked square with an unmarked square, right sides together. Sew on the marked line all the way around the star. Trim ¼" from the stitching line. Clip the inner and outer points. Cut a 1" slit in the center of one layer *only*. Turn the star right side out through the slit. Push out the points and smooth the seams. Press the star flat. Whipstitch the slit closed. Make a total of four stars.

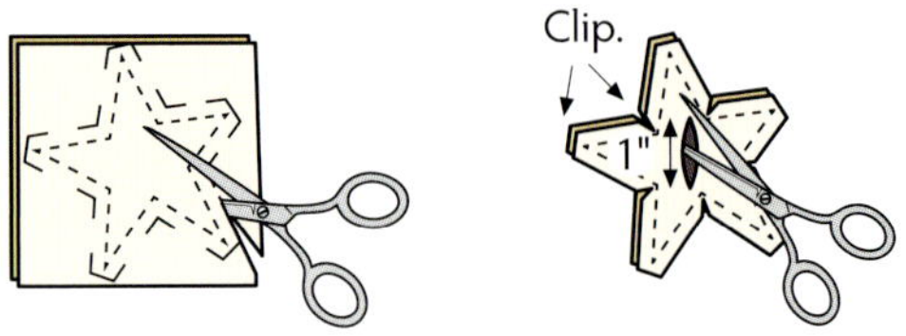

Make 4.

finishing the place mats

If you need detailed instructions about any of the finishing steps, download free information at ShopMartingale.com/HowtoQuilt.

1 Layer a backing rectangle, batting rectangle, and place-mat top. Baste the layers together. Repeat to make a total of four layered pieces.

2 Quilt each place mat by hand or machine. The mats shown are quilted in a 1" grid.

3 Using the 2"-wide red print #1 strips, make the binding and attach it to each place mat.

4 Position a stocking on the beige rectangle of each place mat as shown. Topstitch around the stocking, leaving the top edge open. Appliqué a star to the top of each tree using matching thread.

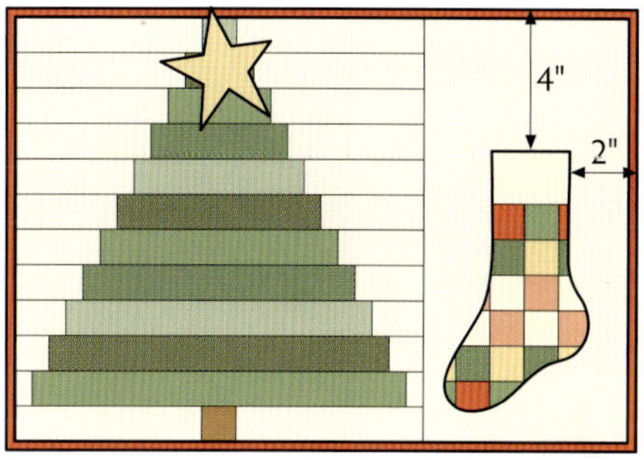

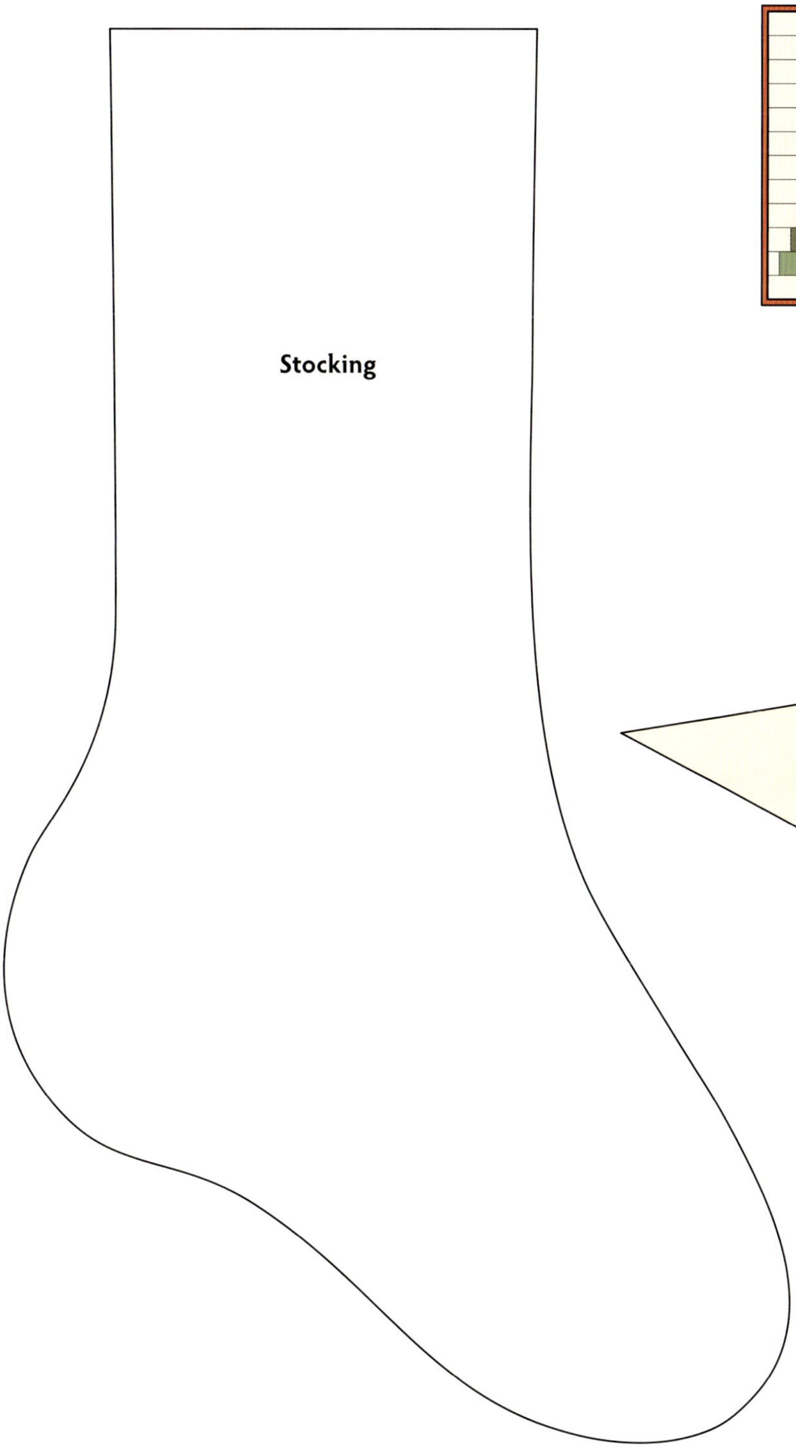

Patterns do not include seam allowances.

slim the snowman runner

This fellow may not be your typical round snowman, but he's long on cheer. Dress him up in a felted wool scarf and top hat and watch the magic happen!

materials

Yardage is based on 42"-wide fabric.

⅓ yard of green print for background and border

¼ yard of mottled tan print or tea-dyed muslin for snowman

5" × 5" square of black felted wool for hat

1" × 2½" rectangle of orange felted wool for nose

¾" × 36" strip of red felted wool for scarf

¼ yard of black solid for binding

⅜ yard of fabric for backing

12" × 42" piece of batting

Lightweight paper-backed fusible web

#8 pearl cotton in colors to match wools

Size 24 chenille needle

2 black snap sets, ⅜" diameter, for eyes

6 black snap sets, ¼" diameter, for mouth

5 black buttons, 1" to 1½" diameter, for body

cutting

All measurements include ¼"-wide seam allowances.

From the green print, cut:

- 3 strips, 1½" × 42"; crosscut into:
    - 2 strips, 1½" × 31½"
    - 1 rectangle, 1½" × 6½"
    - 12 squares, 1½" × 1½"
- 1 rectangle, 5" × 6½"

From the tan print, cut:

- 1 strip, 4½" × 42"; crosscut into:
    - 2 rectangles, 4½" × 14"
    - 1 square, 4½" × 4½"

From the black solid, cut:

- 3 strips, 2½" × 42"

assembling the runner top

Use a ¼" seam allowance. Press the seam allowances as indicated by the arrows.

1 Draw a diagonal line from corner to corner on the wrong side of each green 1½" square. Place a marked square on each corner of the tan 4½" square as shown, right sides together. Sew on the marked lines. Trim ¼" from the stitching lines. Press. In the same manner, add a marked square to each corner of both muslin 4½" × 14" rectangles.

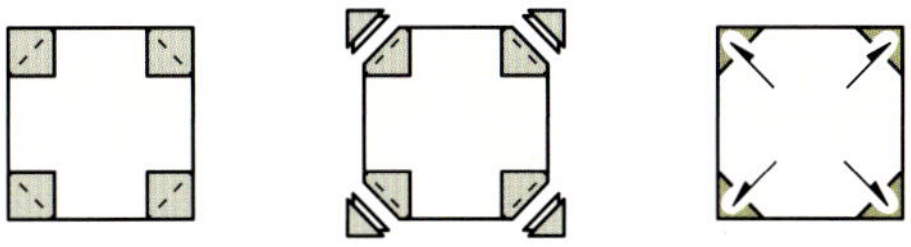

Make 1 block, 4½" × 4½".

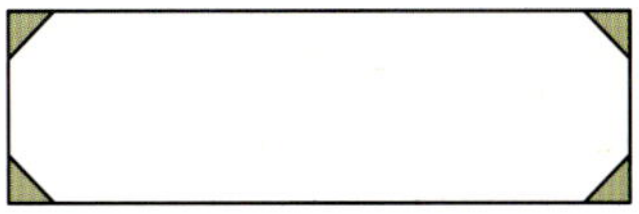

Make 2 blocks, 4½" × 14".

FINISHED RUNNER
6½" × 37"

2 Refer to the runner assembly diagram below to join the units from step 1 in one vertical row. Press. The runner top should measure 4½" × 31½", including seam allowances.

3 Sew the green 1½" × 31½" strips to the sides of the runner top. Press. Join the green 5" × 6½" rectangle to the top edge of the runner and the green 1½" × 6½" rectangle to the bottom edge of the runner. Press. The runner top should measure 6½" × 37", including seam allowances.

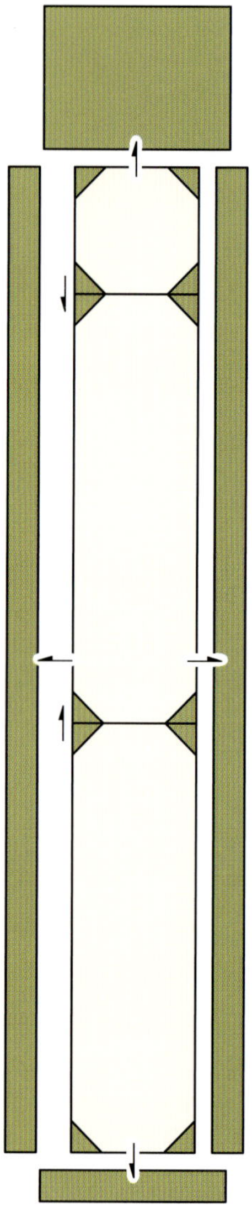

Runner assembly

finishing the runner

If you need detailed instructions about any of the finishing steps, download free information at ShopMartingale.com/HowtoQuilt.

1. Layer the backing, batting, and runner top. Baste the layers together.
2. Quilt by hand or machine. The runner shown is quilted with horizontal lines spaced 1" apart.
3. Using the black 2½"-wide strips, make the binding and attach it to the runner.
4. Using the patterns below and referring to "Fusible-Web Appliqué" on page 78, prepare the appliqués.
5. Refer to the appliqué placement guide at right to fuse the wool shapes in place. With one strand of matching pearl cotton and the chenille needle, whipstitch around each shape. Separate the snap sets into male and female halves; discard or set aside the female halves for another project. Using black pearl cotton, stitch the ⅜" male snap halves to the snowman's face for the eyes and the ¼" male snap halves to the snowman's face for the mouth. Stitch the buttons to the snowman body.
6. Make five 1"-long cuts on each end of the red wool strip to resemble fringe. Fold the strip in half widthwise. With the fold on the left edge of the snowman's neck, pin the scarf in place. Using matching pearl cotton, whipstitch the edges in place along the neck only. Tie the scarf in a knot on the right edge of the snowman's neck and let the ends of the scarf hang loose.

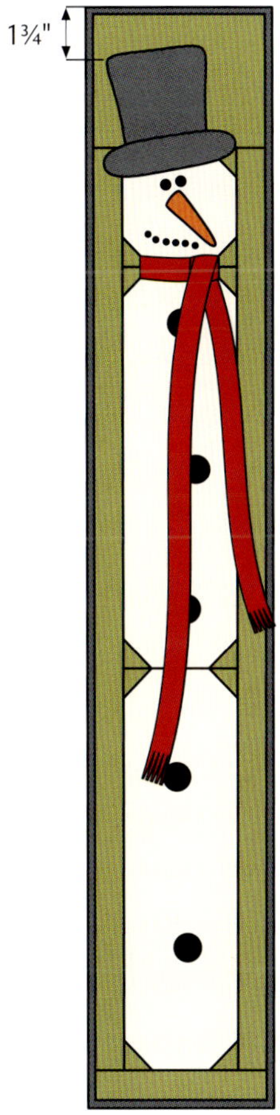

Appliqué placement guide

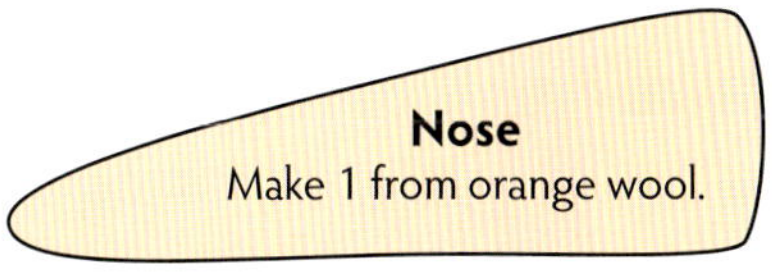

Patterns do not include seam allowances and are reversed for fusible appliqué.

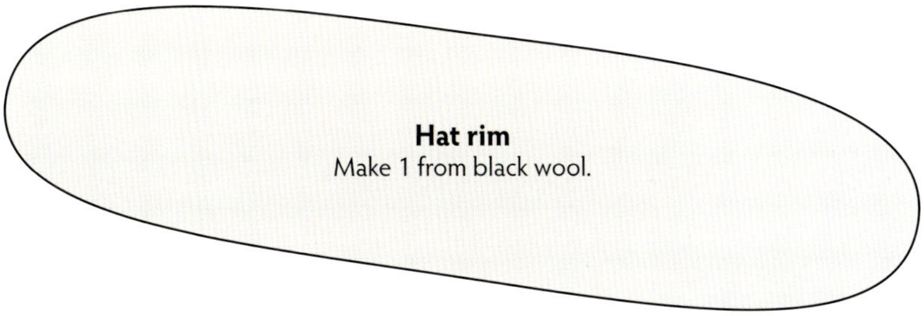

Snow
flakes

snowflakes mini runner

Super quick and easy to sew, a mini runner is perfect for using up small fabric scraps. Extend its use through the winter by picking non-holiday prints for the block corners.

materials

Yardage is based on 42"-wide fabric.

20 squares, 1¾" × 1¾", of assorted medium to dark prints in Christmas colors for blocks (collectively referred to as "darks")

5 squares, 5" × 5", of assorted light prints for blocks

¼ yard of black solid for embroidered rectangles and binding

2" × 4" rectangle of orange felted wool for noses

⅓ yard of fabric for backing

9" × 27" piece of batting

White fine-tip pen to transfer embroidery designs (I used a Sakura Gelly Roll pen) or Glad Press'n Seal plastic wrap

6-strand embroidery floss in ecru, orange, and black

Size 7 embroidery needle

Lightweight paper-backed fusible web

4 black buttons, ½" diameter, for eyes

9 black buttons, ⅛" diameter, for eyes and mouths

4 black snap sets, ⅜" diameter, for eyes

cutting

All measurements include ¼"-wide seam allowances.

From *each of 2* of the assorted light print squares, cut:

- 1 rectangle, 3½" × 5" (2 total)

From the black solid, cut:

- 2 strips, 2½" × 42"
- 1 rectangle, 2" × 5"
- 1 rectangle, 1½" × 5"

making the blocks

Use a ¼" seam allowance. Press the seam allowances as indicated by the arrows.

1 Draw a diagonal line from corner to corner on the wrong side of each dark 1¾" square. Place a marked square on each corner of a light 5" square as shown, right sides together. Sew on the lines. Trim ¼" from the stitching lines. Press. Repeat to make a total of three blocks measuring 5" square, including seam allowances. In the same manner, sew the remaining marked squares to each corner of the light 3½" × 5" rectangles to make two blocks measuring 3½" × 5", including seam allowances.

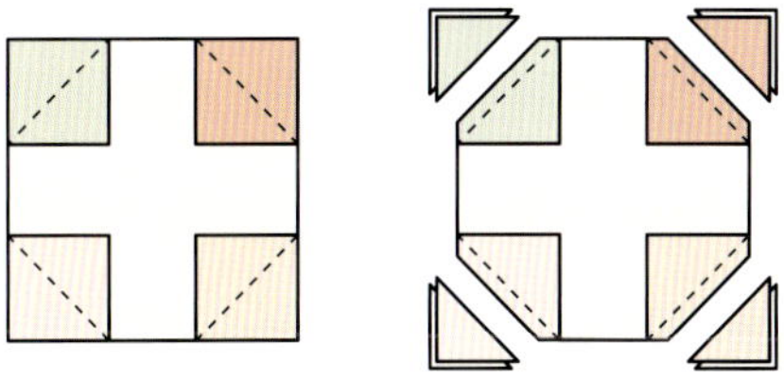

Make 3 blocks, 5" × 5".

Make 2 blocks, 3½" × 5".

FINISHED MINI RUNNER
22½" × 5"

FINISHED BLOCKS
4½" × 4½", 4½" × 3", and 3" × 4½"

2 Sew the black 2" × 5" rectangle to one long edge of a 3½" × 5" block to make a block measuring 5" square, including seam allowances. Press.

Make 1 block, 5" × 5".

assembling and embroidering the runner top

1 Lay out the blocks and black 1½" × 5" rectangle as shown. Sew the blocks and rectangle together. Press. The runner top should measure 22½" × 5".

Runner assembly

2 Using a light box or window, the white marking pen, and the patterns on page 39, carefully transfer the word *snow* to the vertical black rectangle and *flakes* to the horizontal black rectangle or use the Glad Press'n Seal method (page 9) to transfer markings. If you have trouble seeing the letters through the dark fabric, trace over the lines on the pattern with a black marker. Using three strands of ecru floss and the embroidery needle, refer to "Embroidery Stitches" on page 79 to backstitch the words.

finishing the runner

If you need detailed instructions about any of the finishing steps, download free information at ShopMartingale.com/HowtoQuilt.

1 Layer the backing, batting, and runner top. Baste the layers together.

2 Quilt by hand or machine. The runner shown is quilted in the ditch of the seams.

3 Using the black 2½"-wide strips, make the binding and attach it to the runner.

4 Using the pattern on page 39 and referring to "Fusible-Web Appliqué" on page 78, prepare the nose appliqués for each snowman's face.

5 Refer to the placement guides on page 39 to fuse the noses in place. With two strands of orange floss and the embroidery needle, whipstitch around each shape.

6 Separate the snap sets into male and female halves; discard or set aside the female halves for another project. Using one strand of black floss, refer to the placement guides to stitch the male snap halves and the buttons to the snowmen's faces for the eyes and mouths.

7 Refer to "Embroidery Stitches" and the placement guides to embroider the remaining mouths using three strands of black floss.

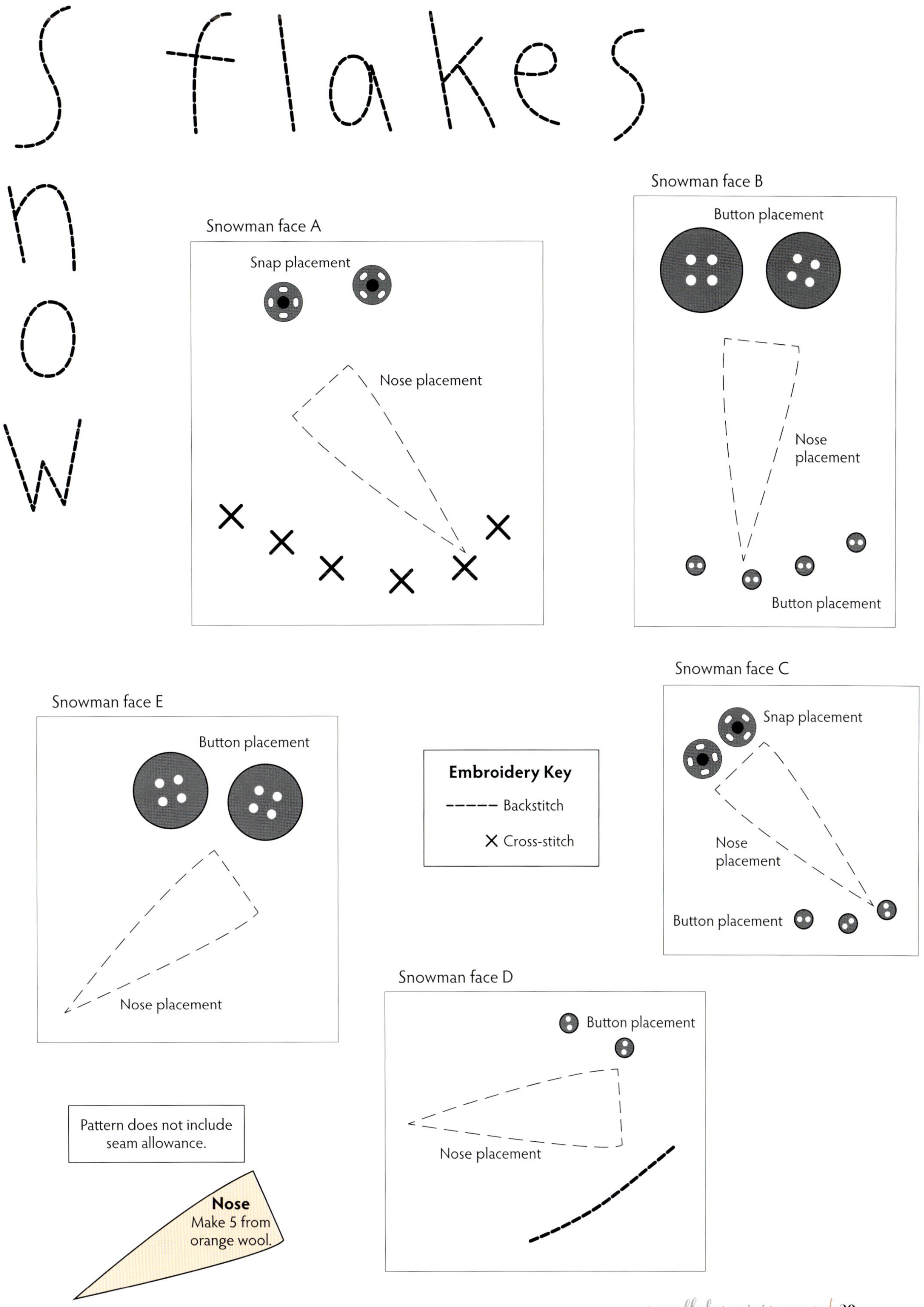
Snowflakes
Snowman face A
Snap placement
Nose placement
Snowman face B
Button placement
Nose placement
Button placement
Snowman face E
Button placement
Nose placement
Embroidery Key
Backstitch
Cross-stitch
Snowman face C
Snap placement
Nose placement
Button placement
Snowman face D
Button placement
Nose placement
Pattern does not include seam allowance.
Nose
Make 5 from orange wool.

tree-trimming party quilt

Do you see what I see? A blizzard of tiny snowman faces dot the garland around the festive tree-trimming fellow in the center.

materials

Yardage is based on 42"-wide fabric.

⅞ yard of black print #1 for quilt-center background and pieced border

¼ yard *each* of 6 assorted green prints for tree and binding

3" × 3" square of brown print for tree trunk

⅝ yard of black print #2 for inner and outer borders

¼ yard of mottled tan print or tea-dyed muslin for middle pieced border

6" × 9" rectangle of ecru houndstooth felted wool for snowman

Scraps of assorted orange felted wools for snowman noses

½" × 12" strip of tan felted wool for snowman arms

½" × 20" strip of red plaid felted wool for scarf

5" × 5" square of gold felted wool for star

1⅓ yards of fabric for backing

43" × 43" square of batting

Lightweight paper-backed fusible web

#8 pearl cotton in black, gold, ecru, red, and tan

6-strand embroidery floss in orange

Size 7 embroidery needle

Size 24 chenille needle

13 assorted buttons, ½" to ¾" diameter, for tree ornaments

2 black snap sets, ¼" diameter, for eyes

3 black snap sets, ½" diameter, for buttons

cutting

All measurements include ¼"-wide seam allowances.

From the brown print, cut:

- 1 square, 2½" × 2½" (LL)

From black print #2, cut:

- 8 strips, 2½" × 42"; crosscut into:
  - 2 strips, 2½" × 20½"
  - 2 strips, 2½" × 24½"
  - 2 strips, 2½" × 32½"
  - 2 strips, 2½" × 36½"

From the tan print, cut:

- 5 strips, 1½" × 42"

From the red wool, cut:

- 2 strips, ½" × 10"

Continued on page 42

Continued from page 41

From black print #1, cut:

- 4 strips, 2½" × 42"; crosscut into:
    - 2 pieces, 2½" × 9½" (S)
    - 56 squares, 2½" × 2½"
- 11 strips, 1½" × 42"; crosscut *6 of the strips* into:
    - 2 pieces, 1½" × 9½" (A)
    - 2 pieces, 1½" × 9" (B)
    - 2 pieces, 1½" × 8½" (C)
    - 2 pieces, 1½" × 8" (D)
    - 2 pieces, 1½" × 7½" (E)
    - 2 pieces, 1½" × 7" (F)
    - 2 pieces, 1½" × 6½" (G)
    - 2 pieces, 1½" × 6" (H)
    - 2 pieces, 1½" × 5½" (I)
    - 2 pieces, 1½" × 5" (J)
    - 2 pieces, 1½" × 4½" (K)
    - 2 pieces, 1½" × 4" (L)
    - 2 pieces, 1½" × 3½" (M)
    - 2 pieces, 1½" × 3" (N)
    - 2 pieces, 1½" × 2½" (O)
    - 2 pieces, 1½" × 2" (P)
    - 2 squares, 1½" × 1½" (Q)
    - 2 pieces, 1" × 1½" (R)

From *each* of the assorted green prints, cut:

- 1 strip, 2½" × 42" (6 total)
- 1 strip, 1½" × 42" (6 total); randomly crosscut the strips into a *total* of:
    - 1 piece, 1½" × 2½" (T)
    - 1 piece, 1½" × 3½" (U)
    - 1 piece, 1½" × 4½" (V)
    - 1 piece, 1½" × 5½" (W)
    - 1 piece, 1½" × 6½" (X)
    - 1 piece, 1½" × 7½" (Y)
    - 1 piece, 1½" × 8½" (Z)
    - 1 piece, 1½" × 9½" (AA)
    - 1 piece, 1½" × 10½" (BB)
    - 1 piece, 1½" × 11½" (CC)
    - 1 piece, 1½" × 12½" (DD)
    - 1 piece, 1½" × 13½" (EE)
    - 1 piece, 1½" × 14½" (FF)
    - 1 piece, 1½" × 15½" (GG)
    - 1 piece, 1½" × 16½" (HH)
    - 1 piece, 1½" × 17½" (II)
    - 1 piece, 1½" × 18½" (JJ)
    - 1 piece, 1½" × 19½" (KK)

assembling the quilt top

Use a ¼" seam allowance. Press the seam allowances as indicated by the arrows.

1 Arrange the A–LL pieces in 19 rows as shown. Sew the pieces in each row together. Press. Join the rows. Press. The quilt center should measure 20½" square, including seam allowances.

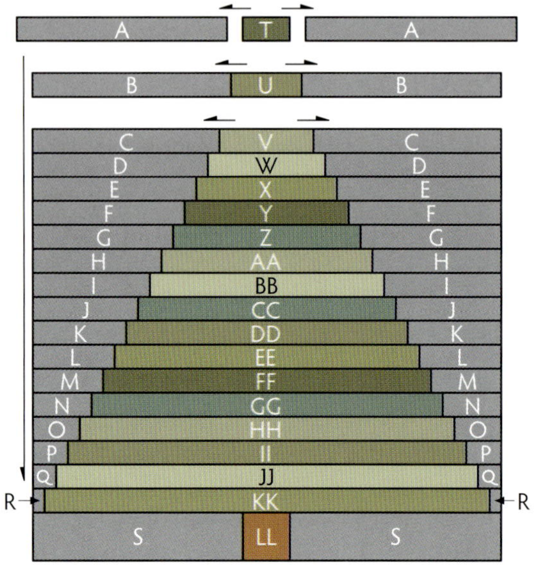

Quilt center,
20½" × 20½"

2 Sew each 1½" × 42" black #1 strip to a tan print 1½" × 42" strip along the long edges to make five strip sets. Press. Crosscut the strip sets into 112 segments, 1½" wide.

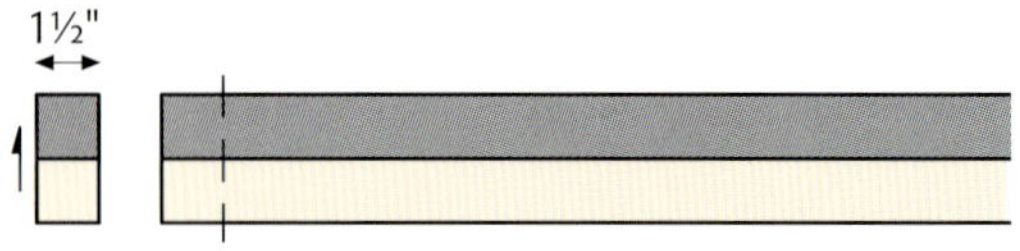

Make 5 strip sets, 2½" × 42".
Cut 112 segments, 1½" × 2½".

3 Join two step 3 segments as shown to make a four-patch unit. Press. Repeat to make a total of 56 four-patch units measuring 2½" square, including seam allowances.

Make 56 units,
2½" × 2½".

4 Lay out two four-patch units and two 2½" black #1 squares in two horizontal rows as shown. Sew the pieces in each row together. Press. Join the rows. Press. Repeat to make a total of 28 Double Four Patch blocks measuring 4½" square, including seam allowances.

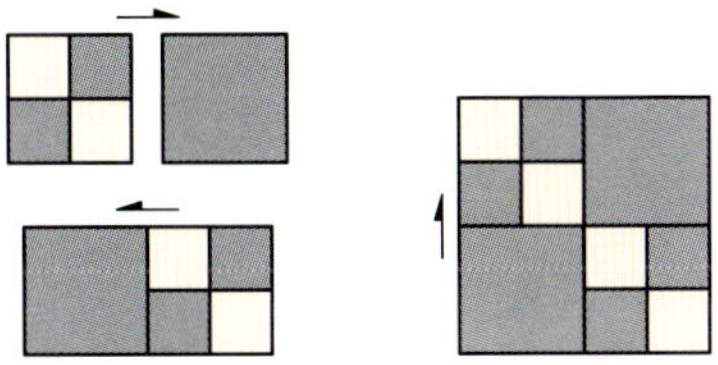

Make 28 blocks, 4½" × 4½".

5 Join six Double Four Patch blocks as shown. Press. Repeat to make a total of two top/bottom middle-border strips measuring 4½" × 24½", including seam allowances. Join eight Double Four Patch blocks as shown. Press. Repeat to make a total of two side middle-border strips measuring 4½" × 32½", including seam allowances.

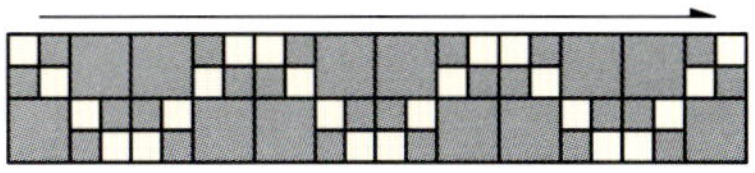

Top/bottom middle border. Make 2, 4½" × 24½".

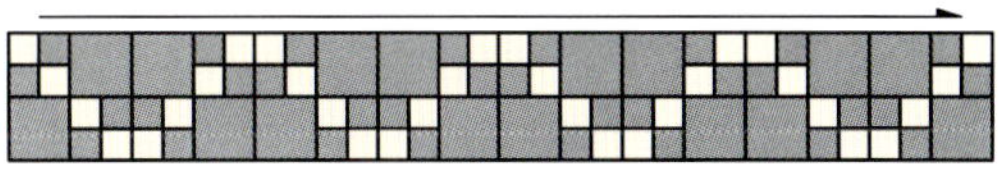

Side middle border. Make 2, 4½" × 32½".

6 Refer to the quilt assembly diagram on page 44 to sew the 2½" × 20½" black #2 inner-border strips to the top and bottom edges of the quilt top. Press. Join the 2½" × 24½" black #2 inner-border strips to the sides of the quilt top. Press. The quilt top should measure 24½" square, including seam allowances.

7 Refer to the quilt assembly diagram below to sew the top/bottom middle-border strips to the top and bottom edges of the quilt top. Press. Join the side middle-border strips to the sides of the quilt top. Press. The quilt top should measure 32½" square, including seam allowances.

8 Sew the 2½" × 32½" black #2 outer-border strips to the top and bottom edges of the quilt top. Press. Join the 2½" × 36½" black #2 outer-border strips to the sides of the quilt top. Press. The quilt top should measure 36½" square.

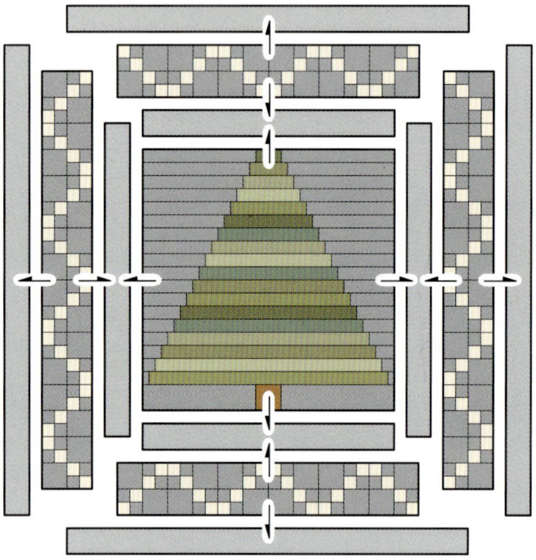

Quilt assembly

finishing the quilt

If you need detailed instructions about any of the finishing steps, download free information at ShopMartingale.com/HowtoQuilt.

1 Layer the backing, batting, and quilt top. Baste the layers together.

2 Quilt by hand or machine. The quilt shown is quilted using black thread in a 2" grid so that the design doesn't interfere with the snowman faces on the middle border.

3 Cut each green 2½" × 42" strip in half to make two strips, 2½" × 21". Randomly join the strips end to end to make the binding; attach it to the quilt.

4 Using the patterns on page 45 and 46 and referring to "Fusible-Web Appliqué" on page 78, prepare the appliqués. For the snowman arms, cut a ½" × 12" strip of fusible web and fuse it to the wrong side of the tan wool. From the prepared strip, cut two strips, ¼" × 5", and two strips, ¼" × 1".

5 Refer to the appliqué and embroidery placement guide on page 45 to fuse the star and the snowman's body, arms, and large nose in place on the quilt top. Referring to "Embroidery Stitches" on page 79 and using matching pearl cotton and the chenille needle, blanket-stitch around the star, body, and arms. Using two strands of orange floss and the embroidery needle, blanket-stitch around the nose.

6 Using red pearl cotton and the chenille needle, whipstitch one end of a red ½" × 10" strip to each side of the snowman's neck. Tie the strips together at the center front of the neck and let the ends hang freely. Make ½"-long cuts ⅛" apart on the strip ends for the fringe.

7 Separate the snap sets into male and female halves; discard or set aside the female halves for another project. Referring to the pattern and using the black pearl cotton and chenille needle, stitch the ¼" male snap halves to the snowman's head for eyes and the ½" male snap halves to the body for buttons.

8 With black pearl cotton, sew a button in the center of the star and another to the snowman's right hand. Randomly sew the remaining buttons to the tree for the ornaments.

9 Refer to the placement guide to fuse the small snowman noses to the middle border. Whipstitch them in place using one strand of orange floss and the embroidery needle. With black pearl cotton and the chenille needle, make a French knot for each snowman eye.

Appliqué and embroidery placement guide

Patterns do not include seam allowances and are reversed for fusible appliqué.

Small nose
Make 25 from assorted orange wools.

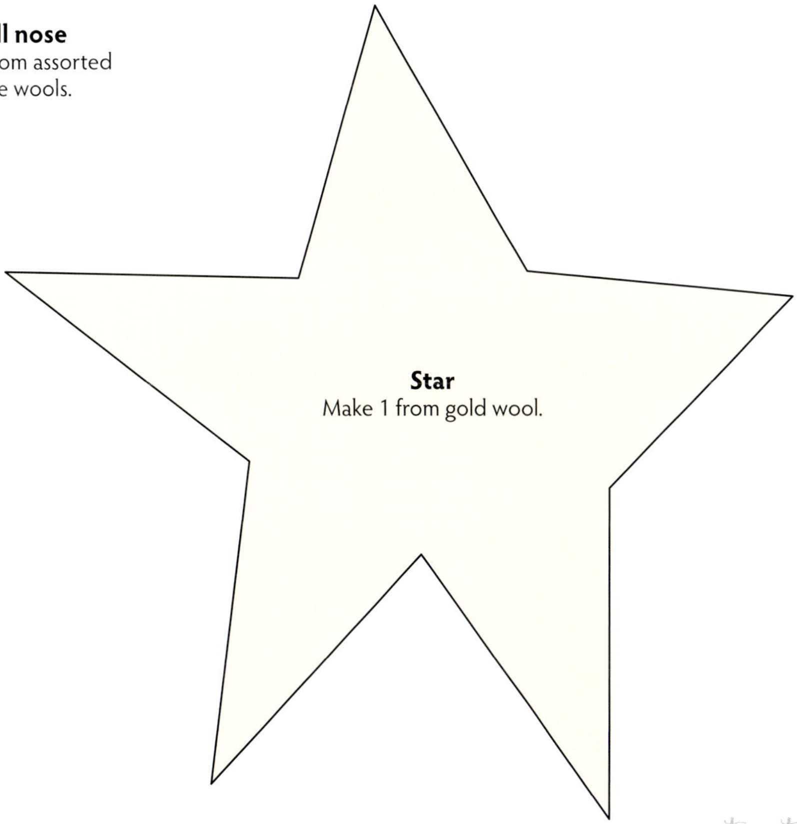

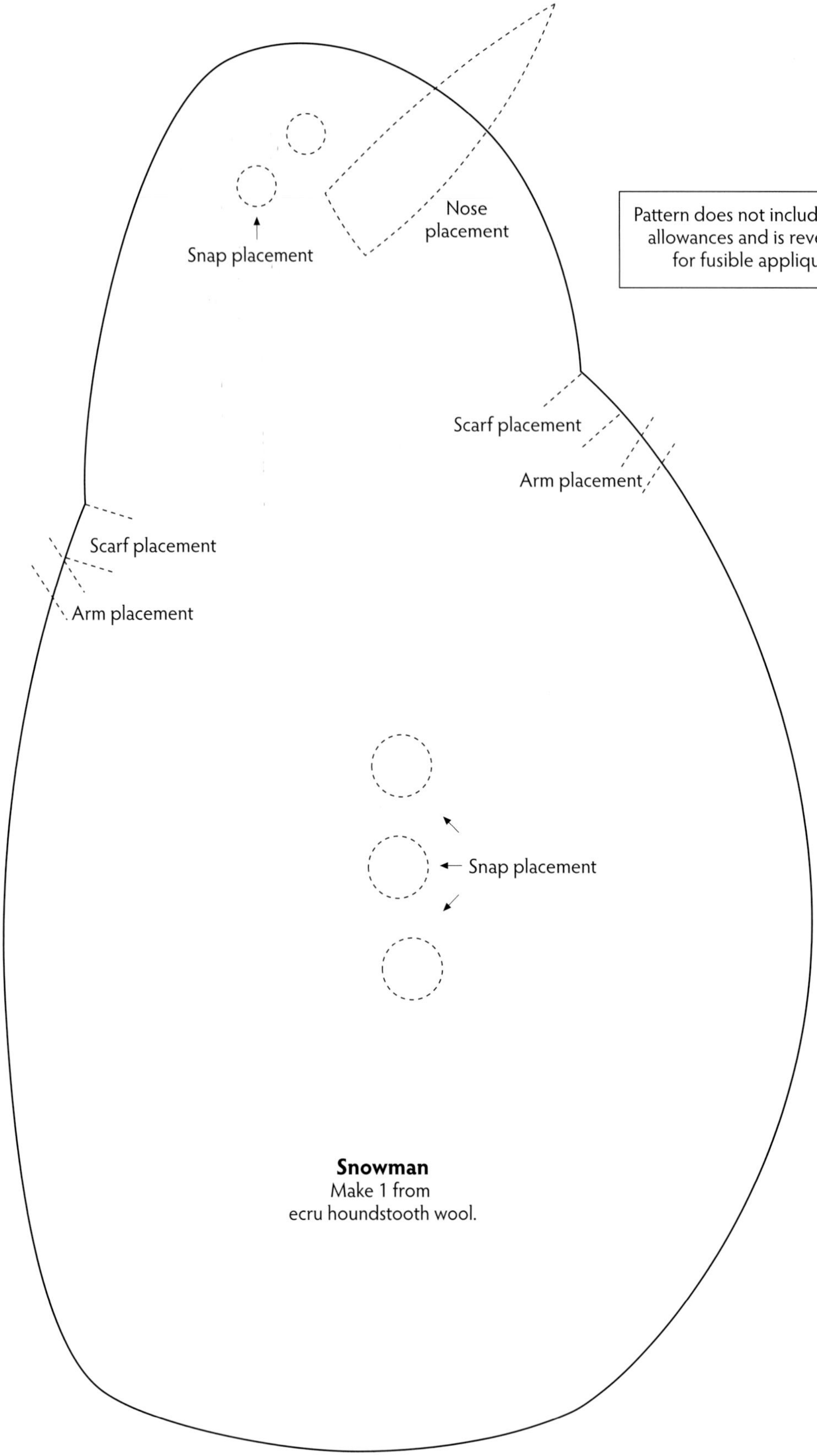

Pattern does not include seam allowances and is reversed for fusible appliqué.

gingerbread candle mat

Pair this quilted mat with a cookie-scented candle to put everyone in the Christmas mood!

materials

Yardage is based on 42"-wide fabric. A fat quarter is 18" × 21".

¼ yard of tan print for background

¼ yard of red print for house and chimneys

3" × 12" strip of brown print for roof

¼ yard of black print for door and binding

6" × 6" square of gold print for windows

4" × 4½" rectangle of black felted wool for shutters

3 rectangles, 3" × 4" *each,* of assorted brown felted wools for gingerbread men

1 fat quarter of fabric for backing

14" × 18" piece of batting

⅓ yard of 1½"-wide brown rickrack

Lightweight paper-backed fusible web

#12 pearl cotton in colors to match wools

Size 7 embroidery needle

6 black buttons, ⅛" diameter, for eyes

6 black buttons, ¼" diameter, for buttons

Water-soluble fabric marker

cutting

All measurements include ¼"-wide seam allowances.

From the tan print, cut:
- 1 rectangle, 4½" × 9½"
- 4 squares, 2" × 2"
- 1 rectangle, 2" × 4½"
- 2 rectangles, 1" × 14"
- 1 rectangle, 1" × 9½"

From the red print, cut:
- 2 rectangles, 4¼" × 6½"
- 1 rectangle, 2" × 3"
- 2 rectangles, 1½" × 2"

From the brown print, cut:
- 1 rectangle, 2" × 9½"

From the black print, cut:
- 2 strips, 2½" × 42"
- 1 rectangle, 2" × 4"

From the gold print, cut:
- 4 rectangles, 2" × 2½"

From the black wool, cut:
- 8 rectangles, ¾" × 1¾"

From the rickrack, cut:
- 1 length, 9½"

assembling the mat top

Use a ¼" seam allowance. Press the seam allowances as indicated by the arrows.

1 To make the chimney section, join two tan 2" squares, two red 1½" × 2" rectangles, and the tan 2" × 4½" rectangle in one horizontal row. Press. The section should measure 2" × 9½", including seam allowances.

Chimney section,
2" × 9½"

2 To make the roof section, draw a diagonal line from corner to corner on the wrong side of the remaining two tan 2" squares. Place a marked square on each end of the brown 2" × 9½" rectangle, right sides together. Sew on the marked line. Trim ¼" from the stitching line. Press. The section should measure 2" × 9½", including seam allowances.

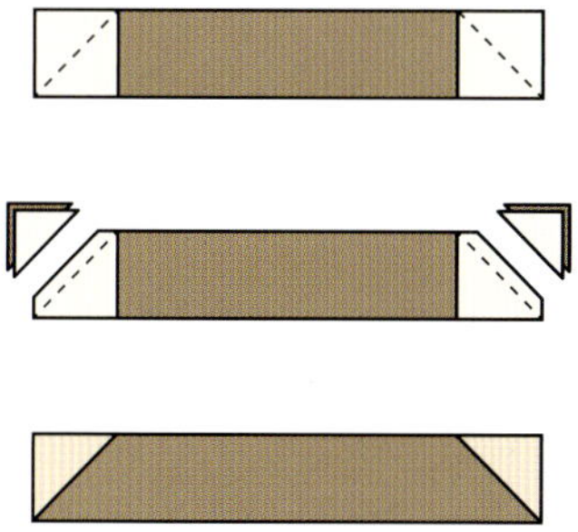

Roof section,
2" × 9½"

3 To make the house section, sew the red 2" × 3" rectangle to the top of the black 2" × 4" rectangle to make the door section. Press. Join a red 4¼" × 6½" rectangle to each side. Press. The house section should be 6½" × 9½", including seam allowances.

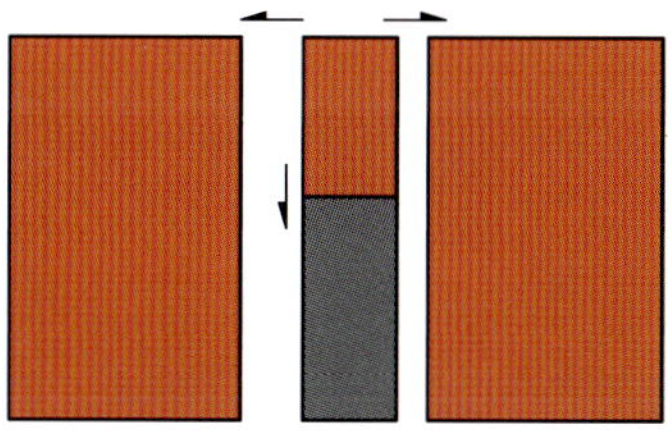

House section,
6½" × 9½"

4 Draw a line ¼" from the top edge of the house section. Align the center of the rickrack over the marked line and pin it in place. With right sides together, sew the roof section to the top of the house section. Trim the excess rickrack from the seam allowance. Press.

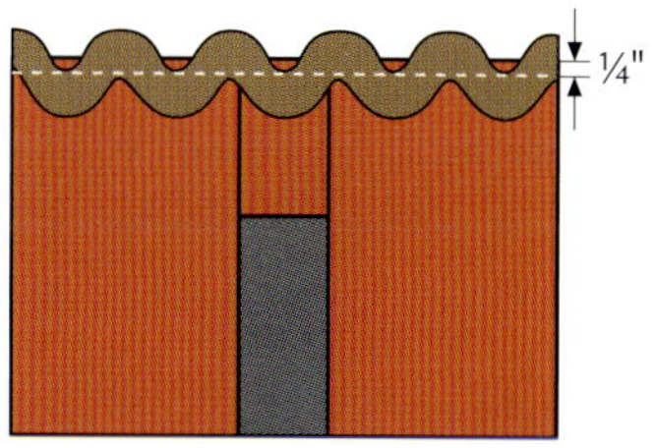

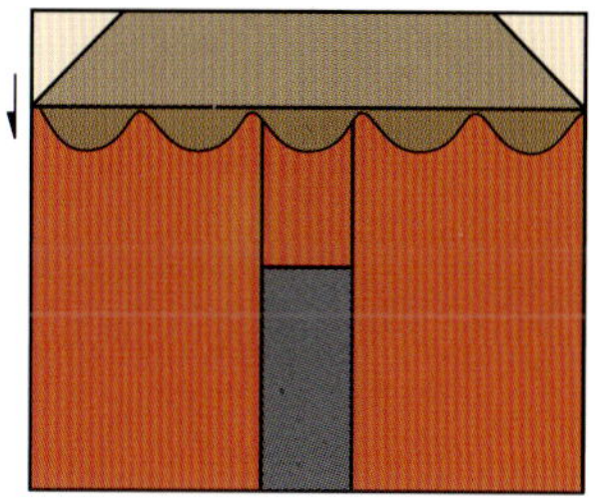

5 Join the chimney section to the top of the roof section. Press. The House block should measure 9½" square, including seam allowances.

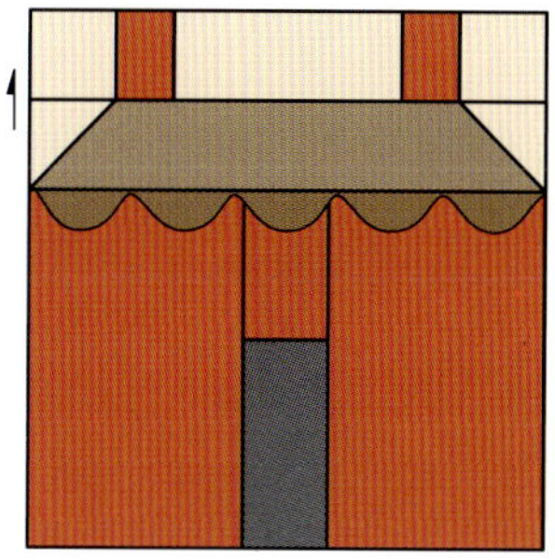

House block,
9½" × 9½"

6 Sew the tan 1" × 9½" rectangle to the top of the House block. Press. Join the tan 4½" × 9½" rectangle to the bottom of the unit. Press. Sew the tan 1" × 14" rectangles to the sides of the unit. Press. The candle-mat top should measure 10½" × 14".

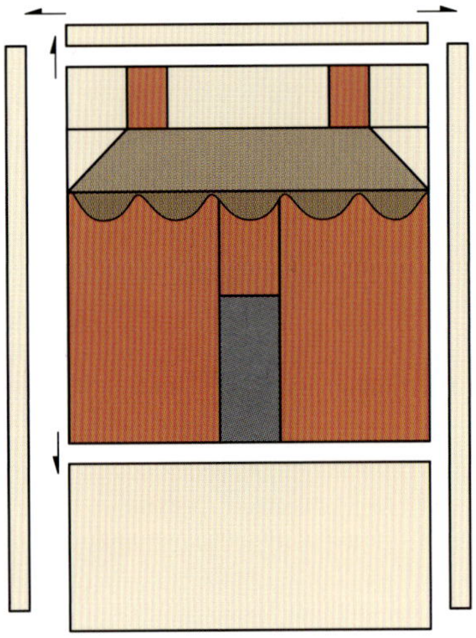

Candle-mat top, 10½" × 14"

finishing the mat

If you need detailed instructions about any of the finishing steps, download free information at ShopMartingale.com/HowtoQuilt.

1 Layer the backing, batting, and candle-mat top. Baste the layers together.

2 Quilt by hand or machine. The mat shown is quilted with an overall meandering pattern.

3 Using the black 2½"-wide strips, make the binding and attach it to the mat.

4 Press under ¼" on the long edges of each gold 2" × 2½" window rectangle. Using matching thread, appliqué the windows to the house along the long edges.

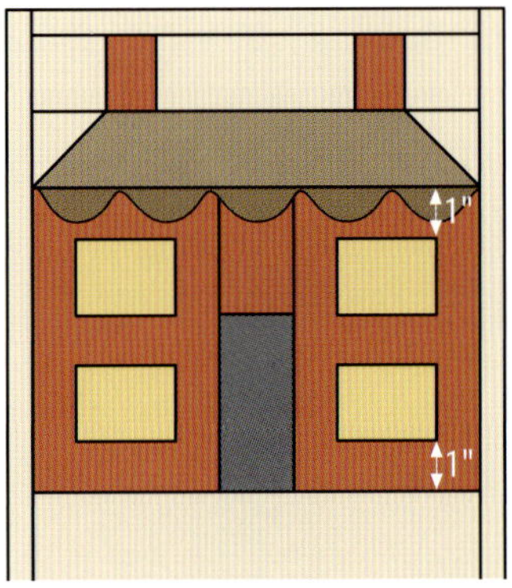

5 Center a black wool ¾" × 1¾" rectangle over the left and right ends of each window, covering the raw edges by ¼". With black pearl cotton, whipstitch the shutters in place.

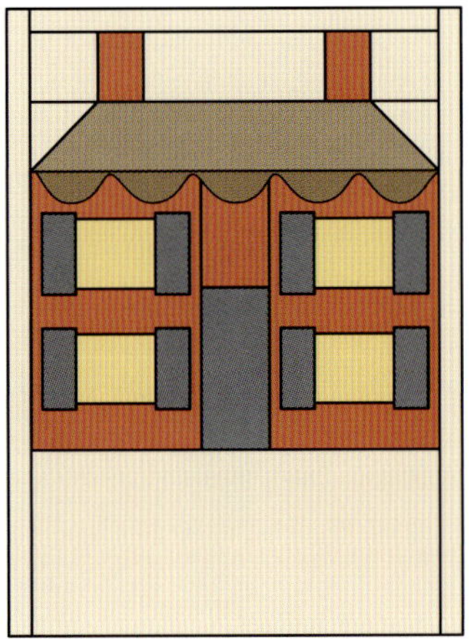

6 Using the patterns on pullout pattern sheet 1 and referring to "Fusible-Web Appliqué" on page 78, prepare the gingerbread men appliqués.

7 Refer to the appliqué placement guide at right to fuse the appliqués in place. Referring to "Embroidery Stitches" on page 79 and using brown pearl cotton and the embroidery needle, whipstitch the appliqués in place. With black pearl cotton, sew the buttons in place.

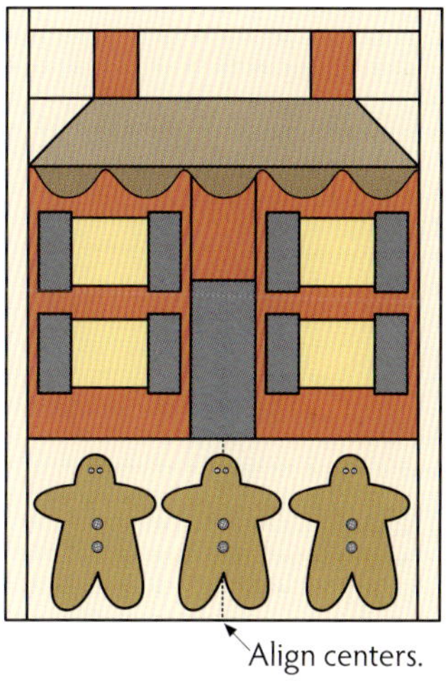

Appliqué placement guide

scrappy snowman quilt

Treasure every tiny scrap as you build this snowman in your sewing room. He's a scrap-saver's delight!

materials

Yardage is based on 42"-wide fabric.

½ yard of mottled tan print or tea-dyed muslin for snowman

1 yard *total* of assorted red prints and solids for background

4" × 4" square of black-and-red print for buttons

½ yard of black Christmas print for border

Scrap of orange felted wool for nose

2½" × 12" strip of brown felted wool for arms

4½" × 18" strip of red-and-cream houndstooth felted wool for scarf

⅜ yard of green print for binding

1¼ yards of fabric for backing

36" × 45" piece of batting

Lightweight paper-backed fusible web

2 black buttons, ¾" diameter, for eyes

#12 pearl cotton in black, brown, and red

Size 7 embroidery needle

cutting

All measurements include ¼"-wide seam allowances.

From the tan print, cut:

- 1 rectangle, 5½" × 7½"
- 2 rectangles, 3½" × 15½"
- 1 rectangle, 3½" × 13½"
- 1 rectangle, 2½" × 13½"
- 1 rectangle, 2½" × 11½"
- 1 rectangle, 2½" × 5½"
- 1 rectangle, 1½" × 11½"
- 1 rectangle, 1½" × 9½"
- 5 rectangles, 1½" × 7½"
- 3 rectangles, 1½" × 5½"
- 1 rectangle, 1½" × 3½"

From the assorted reds, cut a *total* of:

- 438 squares, 1½" × 1½"

From the black-and-red print, cut:

- 3 squares, 1½" × 1½"

From the black Christmas print, cut:

- 4 strips, 3½" × 42"; crosscut into:
    - 2 strips, 3½" × 23½"
    - 2 strips, 3½" × 38½"

From the red-and-cream houndstooth wool, cut:

- 2 strips, 2" × 18"

From the green print, cut:

- 4 strips, 2½" × 42"

assembling the quilt top

Use a ¼" seam allowance. Press the seam allowances as indicated by the arrows.

1 Refer to the quilt center assembly diagram at right to arrange the tan rectangles and red and black-and-red 1½" squares in 32 rows. Sew the squares in the first row together. Press. Sew the squares in the second row together. Press. Join the first and second rows. Press the seam allowances in one direction.

2 Sew the pieces in the third row together. Press. Join the completed row to the previous rows. Press the seam allowances in the same direction as before. Continue in this manner to sew each row together and then add it to the joined rows until the quilt top is complete. The quilt center should measure 23½" × 32½", including seam allowances.

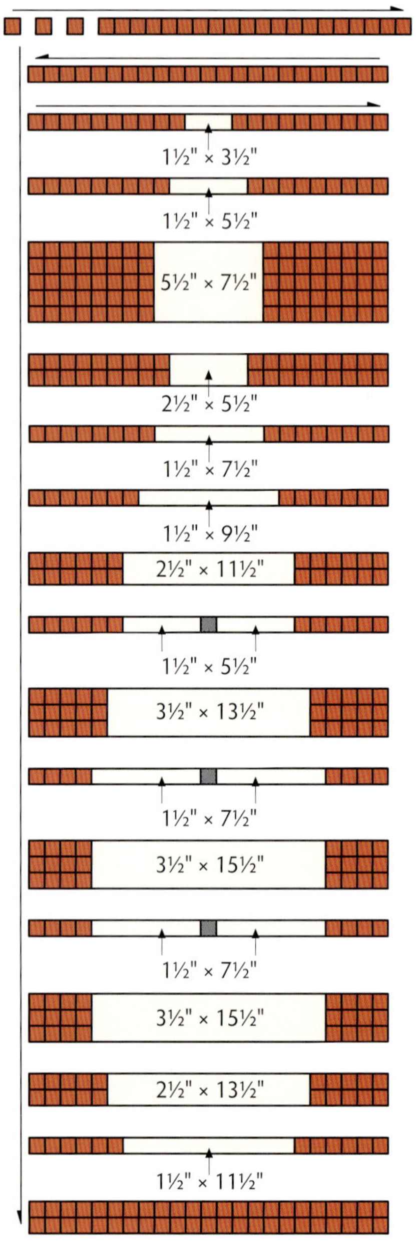

Quilt center assembly

3 Sew the Christmas print 3½" × 23½" strips to the top and bottom of the quilt center. Press seam allowances toward the borders. Join the Christmas print 3½" × 38½" strips to the sides of the quilt top. Press. The quilt top should measure 29½" × 38½".

finishing the quilt

If you need detailed instructions about any of the finishing steps, download free information at ShopMartingale.com/HowtoQuilt.

1. Layer the backing, batting, and quilt top. Baste the layers together.

2. Quilt by hand or machine. The quilt shown is quilted with an allover swirl design.

3. Using the green 2½"-wide strips, make the binding and attach it to the quilt.

4. Refer to "Fusible-Web Appliqué" on page 78 and use the pattern on pullout pattern sheet 1 to prepare one nose from the orange wool.

5. Cut a 2½" × 12" strip of fusible web. Follow the manufacturer's instructions to fuse the strip to the wrong side of the brown wool 2½" × 12" strip. From the fused strip, cut two strips, ½" × 12", and five strips, ½" × 4", for the arms.

6. Refer to the appliqué placement guide, above right, to position the nose and arm pieces; fuse in place. Using black pearl cotton for the nose and brown for the arms, whipstitch in place.

7. Using black pearl cotton, sew the buttons in place for the eyes. With the red pearl cotton, whipstitch one end of a red-and-cream houndstooth wool strip to each side of the neck. Tie the scarf strips together in a knot at the center of the snowman's neck. Make ⅛"-long cuts in the ends of the scarf strips to resemble fringe.

Appliqué placement guide

instant aging

To give your quilt a darker, aged look, brew a large pot of plain black tea. Add instant coffee granules until the desired shade is reached. Test the color by dipping a scrap of fabric in the mixture; let it dry. Add more coffee granules if you want darker fabric. Once the desired color is achieved, dip your quilt in the mixture, remove it from the liquid, and lay the quilt on an old towel. Roll up the quilt in the towel to remove the excess liquid, and then let air-dry. The wetter the quilt, the darker the tea-dyed effect. For an even darker look, dry the piece in the sun.

WATKINS COOK BOOK
Pin Wheel Fruit Refrigerator Cookies
Ice Box Cookies
Watkins Fruit Cookies

sugar and spice mini quilt

You'll love how these three little gingerbread men bring your quilt to life. They're practically jumping out of their bowl to wish you and yours a happy holiday!

materials

Yardage is based on 42"-wide fabric. Fat quarters are 18" × 21".

¼ yard of black print for block center squares and binding

6 fat quarters of assorted light prints for blocks

6 fat quarters of assorted dark prints for blocks

½ yard of fabric for backing

17" × 21" piece of batting

4" × 6" rectangle of gold felted wool for bowl

4" × 8" rectangle of brown felted wool for gingerbread men

2" × 2" square of green felted wool for holly leaves

Lightweight paper-backed fusible web

#12 pearl cotton in ecru and colors to match wool

3 red buttons, ¼" diameter, for holly berries

Size 7 embroidery needle

cutting

All measurements include ¼"-wide seam allowances.

From the black print, cut:

- 1 strip, 1½" × 42"; crosscut into 12 squares, 1½" × 1½" (A)
- 2 strips, 2½" × 42"

From the assorted light prints, cut a *total* of:

- 12 rectangles, 1" × 1½" (B)
- 12 rectangles, 1" × 2" (C)
- 12 rectangles, 1" × 2½" (F)
- 12 rectangles, 1" × 3" (G)
- 12 rectangles, 1" × 3½" (J)
- 12 rectangles, 1" × 4" (K)

From the assorted dark prints, cut a *total* of:

- 12 rectangles, 1" × 2" (D)
- 12 rectangles, 1" × 2½" (E)
- 12 rectangles, 1" × 3" (H)
- 12 rectangles, 1" × 3½" (I)
- 12 rectangles, 1" × 4" (L)
- 12 rectangles, 1" × 4½" (M)

making the blocks

Use a ¼" seam allowance. Press the seam allowances as indicated by the arrows.

1 Sew a B rectangle to the top edge of an A square. Press. Add a C rectangle to the left edge of the unit. Press. Add a D rectangle to the bottom edge and then an E rectangle to the right edge to complete the first round, which should measure 2½" square.

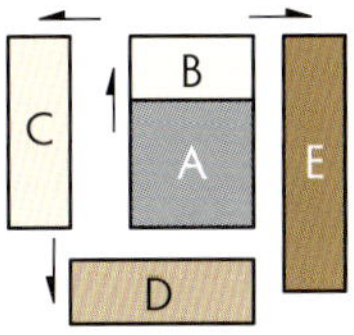

2 Working in a counterclockwise direction, continue adding rectangles F–M to the unit in alphabetical order to complete three rounds. The finished block should measure 4½" square, including seam allowances.

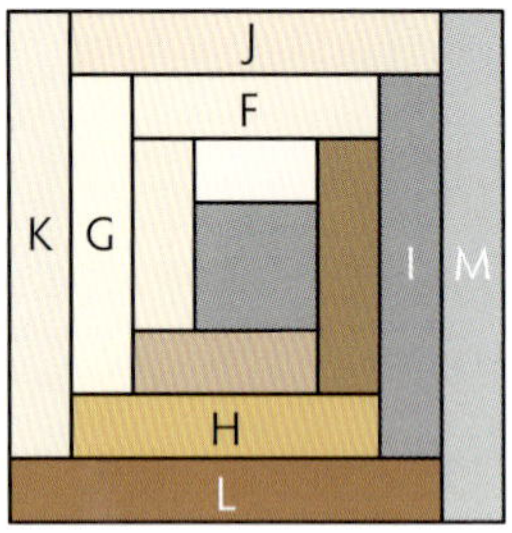

Log Cabin block,
4½" × 4½"

3 Repeat steps 1 and 2 to make a total of 12 blocks.

assembling the quilt top

Referring to the assembly diagram, lay out the blocks in four rows of three blocks each. Join the blocks in each row. Press. Join the rows. Press.

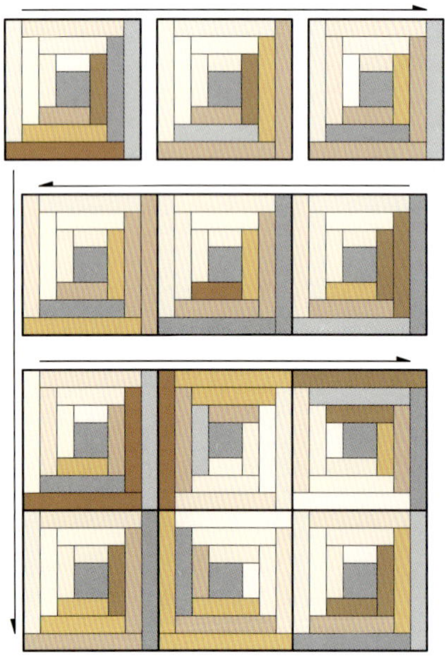

Quilt assembly

finishing the quilt

If you need detailed instructions about any of the finishing steps, download free information at ShopMartingale.com/HowtoQuilt.

1 Layer the backing, batting, and quilt top. Baste the layers together.

2 Quilt by hand or machine. The quilt shown is quilted with a diagonal crosshatch design, with the lines spaced 1½" apart.

3 Using the black 2½"-wide strips, make the binding and attach it to the quilt.

4 Using the patterns on page 59 and referring to "Fusible-Web Appliqué" on page 78, prepare the appliqués.

5 Refer to the appliqué and embroidery placement guide to fuse the appliqués in place. Referring to "Embroidery Stitches" on page 79 and using matching pearl cotton and the embroidery needle, whipstitch the appliqués in place. With the ecru pearl cotton, stem-stitch the lines on the bowl and approximately ⅛" from the edge of each gingerbread man, cross-stitch the buttons, and make French knots for the eyes. Add the buttons atop the holly leaves.

Appliqué and embroidery placement guide

FINISHED MINI QUILT
12½" × 16½"

FINISHED BLOCK
4" × 4"

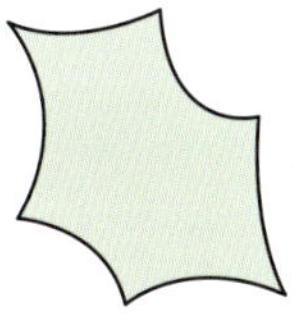

Holly leaf
Make 3 from green wool.

Embroidery Key

- × Cross-stitch
- • French knot
- —— Stem stitch

Patterns do not include seam allowances and are reversed for fusible appliqué.

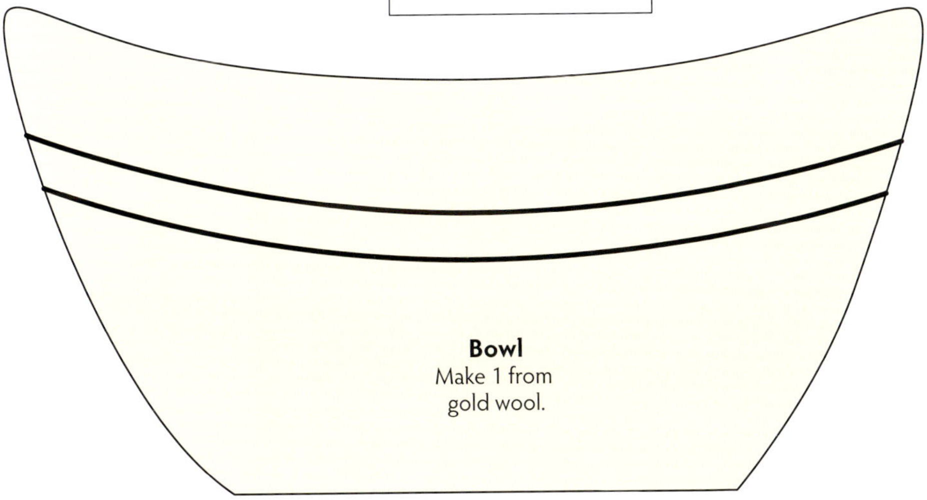

Bowl
Make 1 from gold wool.

Gingerbread man
Make 3 from brown wool.

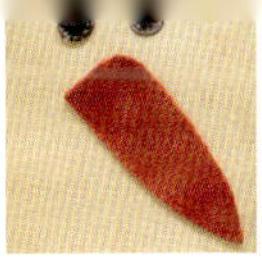

christmas bowl fillers

Tuck a few of these festive creations into a bowl or basket filled with greenery or vintage ornaments to add cheer to any room in the house.

materials

Fat eighths are 9" × 21".

FOR *EACH* BOWL FILLER

Fiberfill stuffing

FOR THE SNOWMAN

1 fat eighth of mottled tan print or tea-dyed muslin for blocks

1 fat eighth of red print for blocks and back

1" × 2" rectangle of orange felted wool for nose

Lightweight paper-backed fusible web

#12 pearl cotton in orange

Size 7 embroidery needle

2 black snap sets or buttons, ¼" diameter, for eyes

2 black buttons, ½" diameter, for body

FOR THE GINGERBREAD MAN

1 fat eighth of mottled tan print or tea-dyed muslin for checkerboard

8 strips, 2" × 6" *each,* of assorted red prints for checkerboard

3" × 4" rectangle of brown felted wool for gingerbread man

Lightweight paper-backed fusible web

⅔ yard of ¾"-wide brown rickrack

#12 pearl cotton in brown and ecru

Size 7 embroidery needle

FOR THE TREE

1 fat eighth of green plaid homespun for tree

Cinnamon stick, 3" long, for trunk

3 rusty jingle bells, 6 mm diameter

Template material

FOR THE PACKAGE

1 fat eighth of beige print for block and back

1 fat eighth of green print for block

1 fat eighth of red print for block

1 black button, ¾" diameter

FOR THE STOCKING

1 fat eighth of mottled tan print or tea-dyed muslin for front and back

2" × 4" rectangle of green felted wool for toe and heel

2" × 5" rectangle of red felted wool for cuff

1" × 1" square of gold felted wool for star

Lightweight paper-backed fusible web

#12 pearl cotton in green, red, and gold

Size 7 embroidery needle

Pipe-cleaner candy cane, 5" long

Real or faux greenery

Template material

cutting

All measurements include ¼"-wide seam allowances.

FOR THE SNOWMAN

From the red print, cut:

- 1 rectangle, 3½" × 9½"
- 12 squares, 1¼" × 1¼"

From the tan print, cut:

- 3 squares, 3½" × 3½"

FOR THE GINGERBREAD MAN

From the tan print, cut:

- 1 square, 4½" × 4½"
- 8 rectangles, 1" × 5"

From *each* of the assorted red prints, cut:

- 1 rectangle, 1" × 5" (8 total)

FOR THE PACKAGE

From the beige print, cut:

- 1 square, 5½" × 5½"
- 4 squares, 1⅞" × 1⅞"
- 4 squares, 1½" × 1½"

From the green print, cut:

- 4 squares, 1⅞" × 1⅞"
- 4 squares, 1½" × 1½"

From the red print, cut:

- 1 rectangle, 1½" × 5½"
- 2 rectangles, 1½" × 2½"

FOR THE STOCKING

From the red wool, cut:

- 1 rectangle, 1¼" × 4"

making the bowl fillers

Use a ¼" seam allowance. Press the seam allowances as indicated by the arrows. Refer to "Fusible-Web Appliqué" on page 78 and the patterns on pages 67 and 68 to prepare the appliqués. Refer to "Embroidery Stitches" on page 79 for information on working the stitches.

SNOWMAN

1 Draw a diagonal line from corner to corner on the wrong side of each red 1¼" square. Place a marked square on each corner of a tan square, right sides together. Sew on the marked lines. Trim ¼" from the stitching lines. Press. Repeat to make a total of three blocks measuring 3½" square, including seam allowances.

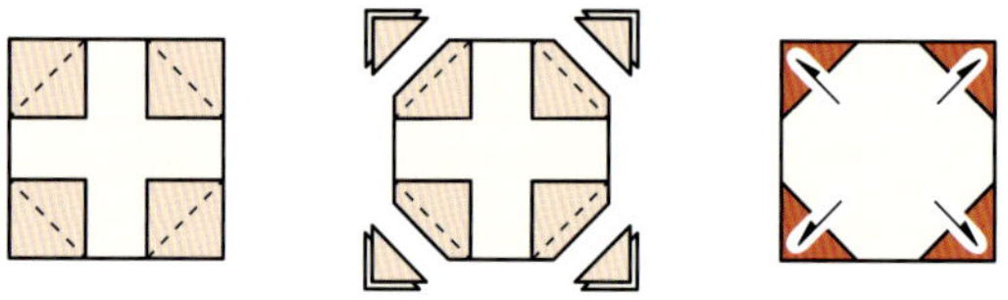

Make 3 blocks,
3½" × 3½".

2 Join the blocks in a vertical column. Press. The snowman front should measure 3½" × 9½", including seam allowances.

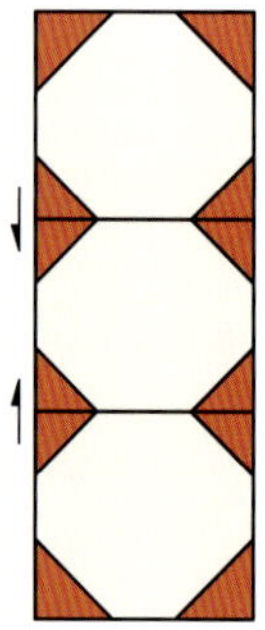

Snowman front,
3½" × 9½"

3 Prepare the nose appliqué. Refer to the appliqué placement guide to fuse the nose to the top block. With orange pearl cotton, whipstitch the nose in place. Sew the male portion of the black ¼"-diameter snaps or the ¼"-diameter buttons in place for the eyes. Sew the black ½"-diameter buttons to the body.

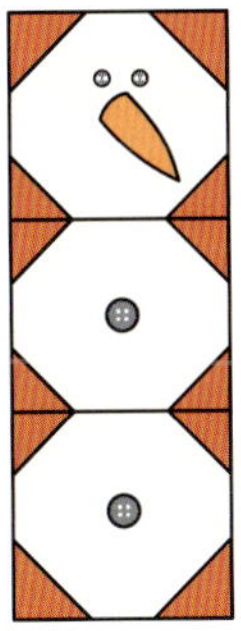

Appliqué placement guide

4 Place the snowman front and red 3½" × 9½" rectangle right sides together. Sew around the layered pieces, leaving a 1½" opening on one long side for turning. Turn the piece right side out. Stuff with fiberfill to the desired fullness. Stitch the opening closed.

GINGERBREAD MAN

1 Alternately sew four tan and four assorted red rectangles together along the long edges to make a strip set. Press the seam allowances toward the red rectangles. Repeat to make a total of two strip sets. Crosscut the strip sets into eight segments, 1" wide.

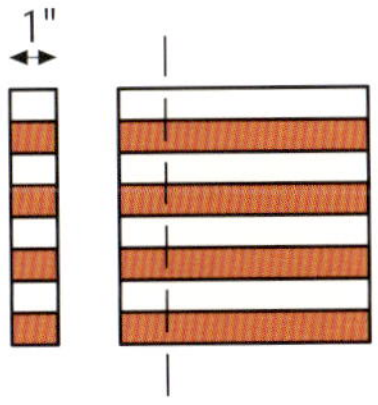

Make 2 strip sets, 4½" × 5".
Cut 8 segments, 1" × 4½".

FINISHED SNOWMAN
3" × 9"

FINISHED GINGERBREAD MAN
4" × 4"

2 Sew the segments together along the long edges, alternating the red and white ends of the strips. The pieced front should measure 4½" square, including seam allowances.

Make 1 front, 4½" × 4½".

3 Make a template using the corner cutting pattern on page 68. Place the template on each corner of the pieced front and the tan 4½" square and mark around it. Cut on the marked lines.

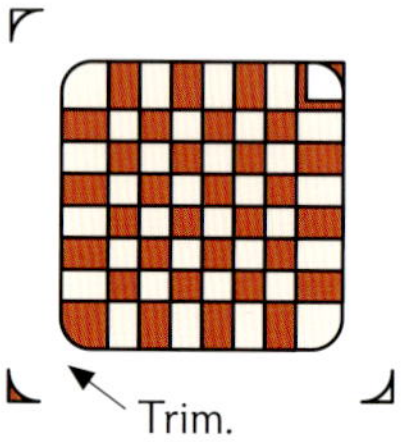

4 Prepare the gingerbread man appliqué using the pattern on page 68. Center the appliqué on the pieced front. With brown pearl cotton, blanket-stitch the man in place. With ecru pearl cotton, stem-stitch the line around the body, make French knots for the eyes, and sew cross-stitches for the buttons.

Appliqué placement guide

5 Pin the rickrack to the right side of the appliquéd front, aligning the center of the trim ¼" from the edges. Baste the rickrack in place, sewing ⅛" from the unit edges. Trim the rickrack even with the unit edges.

6 Pin the front and tan 4½" backing squares right sides together. Sew around the layered squares, leaving a 2" opening along the bottom for turning. Turn the piece right side out. Stuff with fiberfill to the desired fullness. Stitch the opening closed.

TREE

1 Trace the treetop pattern on page 68 onto template material and cut it out. Using the pattern, cut two treetops from the green plaid homespun. Place the pieces right sides together and sew around the shapes, leaving a 1½" opening along the bottom for turning. Turn the piece right side out.

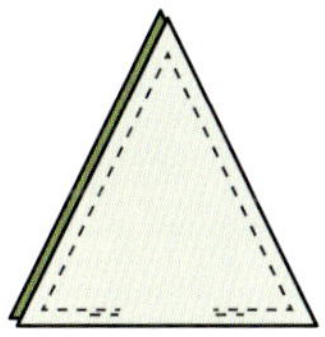

2 Stuff the treetop to the desired fullness. Insert the cinnamon stick to a depth of approximately ½" into the opening. Stitch the opening closed around the cinnamon stick to hold it in place.

3 Sew a bell to each point of the tree.

PACKAGE

1 Draw a diagonal line from corner to corner on the wrong side of each beige 1⅞" square. Place a marked square on top of a green square, right sides together. Sew ¼" from both sides of the marked line. Cut the squares apart on the marked line to make two half-square-triangle units. Press. Repeat to make a total of eight units measuring 1½" square, including seam allowances.

Make 8 units, 1½" × 1½".

2 Arrange two half-square-triangle units, one beige 1½" square, and one green 1½" square in two rows as shown. Sew the pieces in each row together. Press. Join the rows. Press. Repeat to make a total of four units measuring 2½" square, including seam allowances.

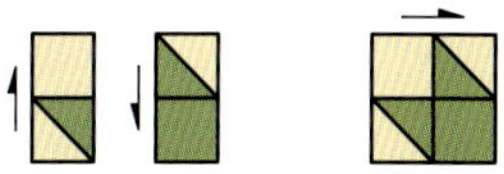

Make 4, 2½" × 2½".

3 Arrange the step 2 units, the red 1½" × 2½" rectangles, and the red 1½" × 5½" rectangle in three rows. Sew the pieces in each row together. Press. Join the rows. Press. The block should measure 5½" square, including seam allowances.

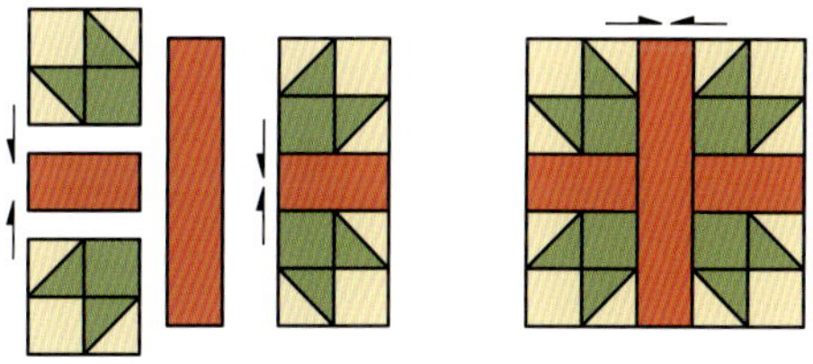

Make 1 block, 5½" × 5½".

4 Place the block and beige 5½" square right sides together. Sew around the layered squares, leaving a 2" opening along the bottom for turning. Turn the piece right side out and stuff to the desired firmness. Stitch the opening closed.

5 Sew the button to the center of the bowl filler, stitching down and back up through all the layers so the button creates an indentation.

FINISHED STOCKING
3⅜" × 5¼"

STOCKING

1 Trace the stocking pattern on page 67 onto template material. Using the pattern, cut two stockings from the tan for the front and back. Transfer the embroidery design to the right side of the front piece. Using green pearl cotton, backstitch the tree trunk and branches. With red pearl cotton, make a French knot at the end of each branch.

2 Using the patterns on page 67, prepare the toe, heel, and star appliqués. Refer to the appliqué placement guide to fuse the shapes to the stocking front. Using matching pearl cotton, whipstitch the star in place and blanket-stitch the inside curve *only* of the heel and toe pieces.

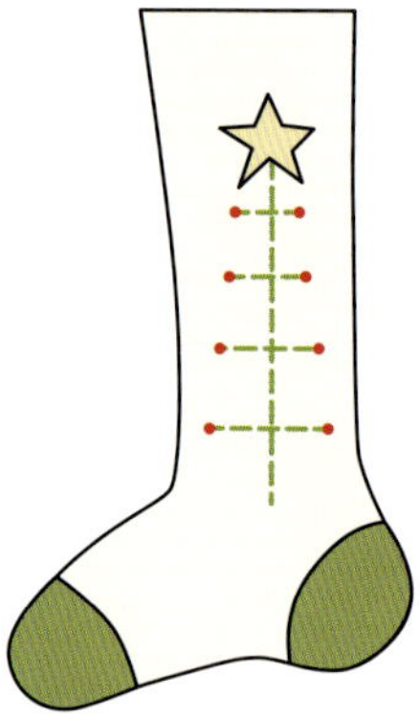

Appliqué placement guide

3 Pin the stocking front and back right sides together. Stitch around the layered pieces, leaving the top open. Clip the curves. Turn the stocking right side out.

4 To make the cuff, fold the red wool rectangle in half widthwise. Sew the short ends together. Press the seam allowances open.

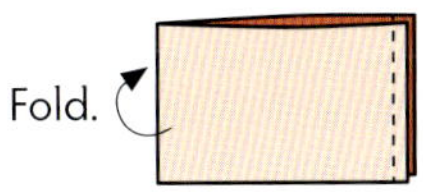

5 Place the cuff inside the stocking, wrong sides together, aligning the top edges and the cuff seam with the heel-side seam. Hand stitch ¼" from the top edge around the stocking. Turn the cuff to the stocking right side, leaving approximately ⅛" inside the stocking so the seamline isn't visible from the right side. Press.

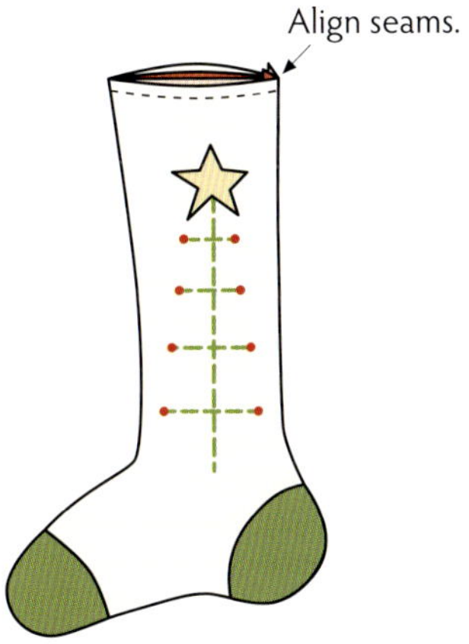

6 Lightly stuff the bottom of the stocking to fill out the toe and heel. Insert the candy cane and some real or faux greenery into the top of the stocking.

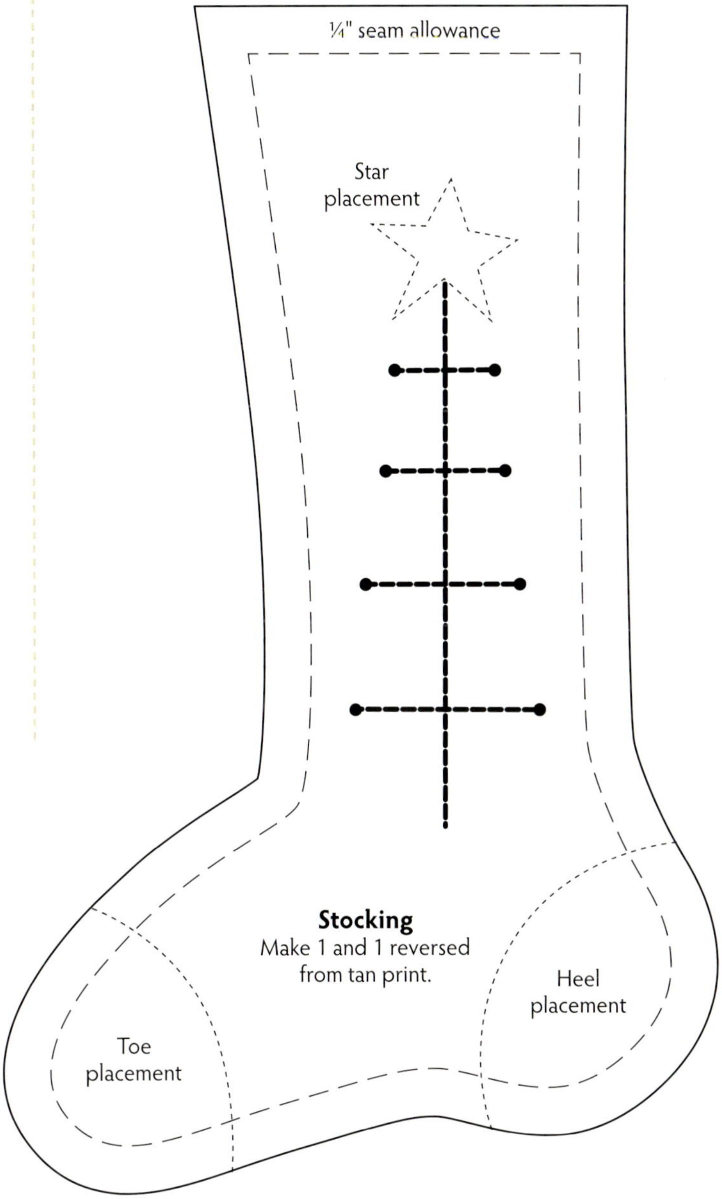

Star, heel, and toe patterns do not include seam allowances and are reversed for fusible appliqué.

Embroidery Key

- - - - - Backstitch

● French knot

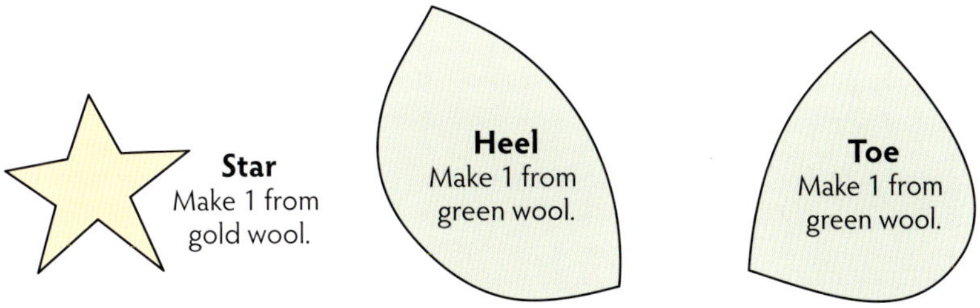

Pattern does not include seam allowances and is reversed for fusible appliqué.

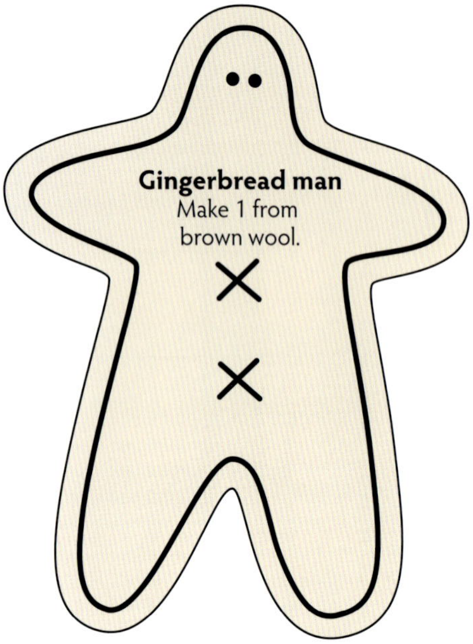

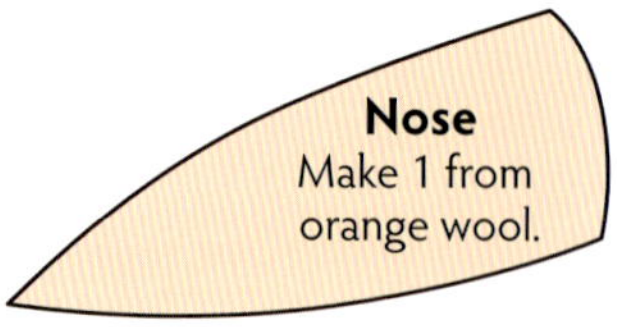

Pattern does not include seam allowances and is reversed for fusible appliqué.

Embroidery Key

- × Cross-stitch
- • French knot
- —— Stem stitch

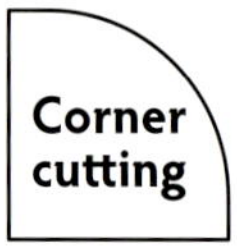

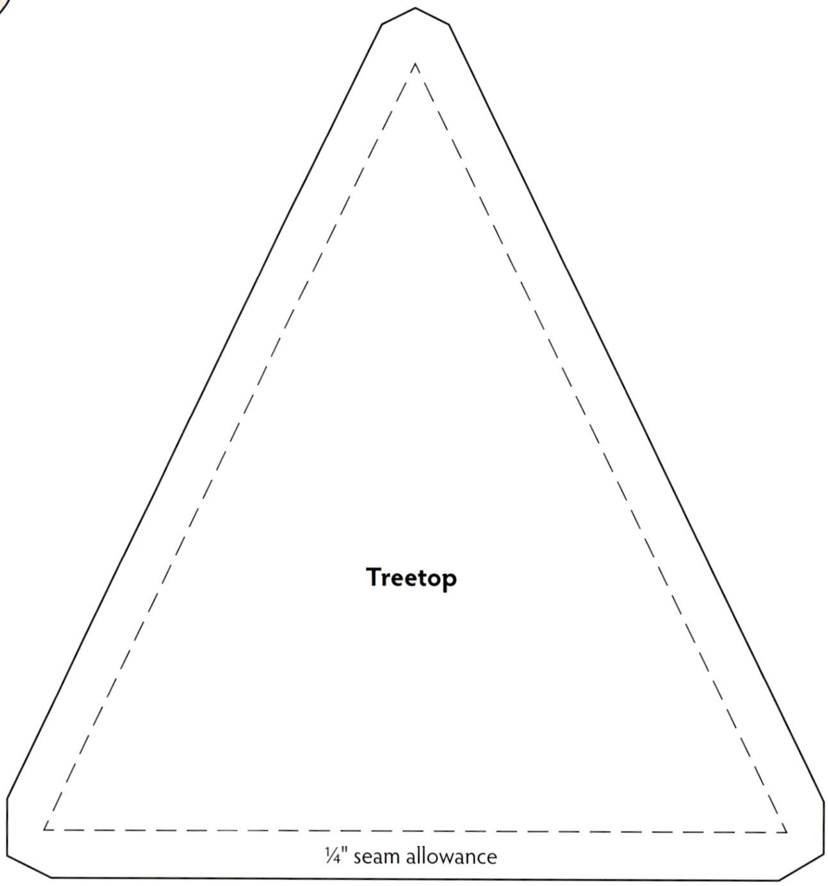

merry mini quilt

Make a special gift fast. Just start stitching, and what to your wondering eyes will appear? A charming quilt that's sure to please anyone you hold dear!

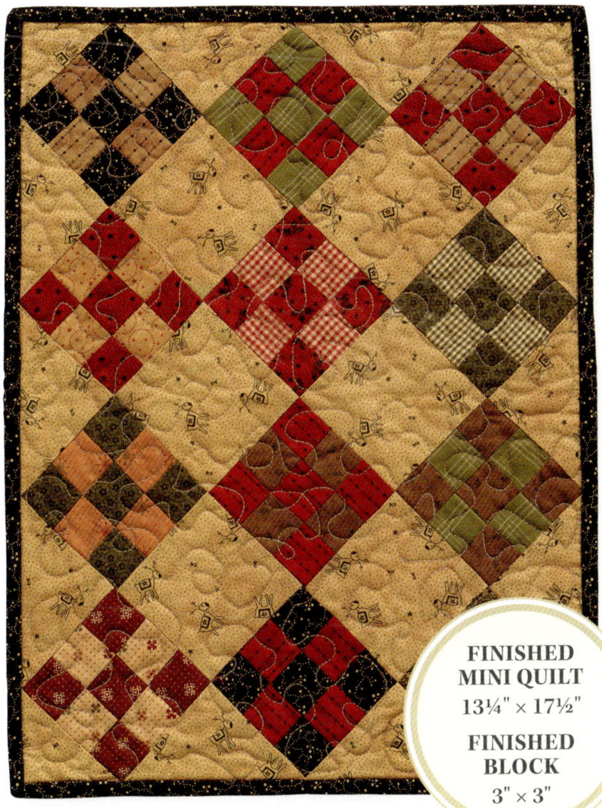

FINISHED MINI QUILT
13¼" × 17½"

FINISHED BLOCK
3" × 3"

materials

Yardage is based on 42"-wide fabric. Fat eighths are 9" × 21".

1 fat eighth *each* of 12 assorted Christmas prints in reds, greens, golds, browns, and blacks for blocks

⅓ yard of tan print for setting squares and triangles

¼ yard of black print for binding

½ yard of fabric for backing

18" × 22" piece of batting

cutting

All measurements include ¼"-wide seam allowances.

CUTTING FOR 1 BLOCK (CUT 12 TOTAL.)

From one Christmas print, cut:

- 5 squares, 1½" × 1½"

From a different Christmas print, cut:

- 4 squares, 1½" × 1½"

CUTTING FOR SETTING PIECES AND BINDING

From the tan print, cut:

- 3 squares, 5½" × 5½"; cut into quarters diagonally to make 12 side setting triangles (you'll have 2 left over)
- 6 squares, 3½" × 3½"
- 2 squares, 3" × 3"; cut in half diagonally to make 4 corner setting triangles

From the black print, cut:

- 2 strips, 2½" × 42"

assembling the quilt top

Use a ¼" seam allowance. Press the seam allowances as indicated by the arrows.

1 Lay out the squares for one block in three rows of three squares each, alternating the two colors. Sew the squares in each row together. Press. Join the rows. Press. Repeat to make a total of 12 blocks measuring 3½" square, including seam allowances.

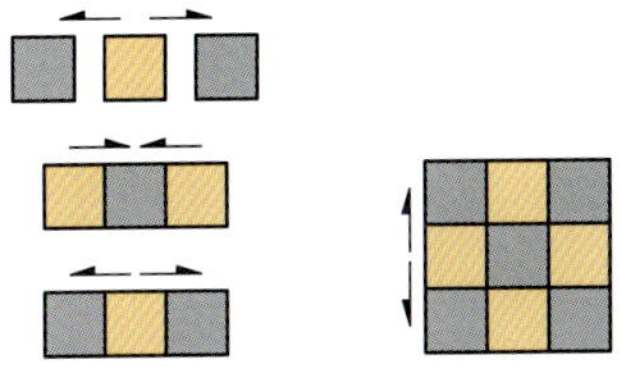

Make 12 blocks, 3½" × 3½".

2 Refer to the quilt assembly diagram to arrange the blocks and tan setting pieces in diagonal rows. Sew the blocks and side setting triangles together in each row. Press. Join the rows. Press. Add the corner triangles last. Press. The quilt top should measure 13¼" × 17½".

Quilt assembly

finishing the quilt

If you need detailed instructions about any of the finishing steps, download free information at ShopMartingale.com/HowtoQuilt.

1 Layer the backing, batting, and quilt top. Baste the layers together.

2 Quilt by hand or machine. The quilt shown is machine quilted with an overall meandering pattern.

3 Using the black 2½"-wide strips, make the binding and attach it to the quilt.

mistletoe ornament

Legend has it that a kiss is promised to all who pass beneath the mistletoe. Make a few of these sprigs to hang around the house and see if it's true!

materials

2 squares, 7" × 7", of different green felted wools for leaves

½" × 12" strip of red felted wool for bow

22-gauge rusty tin wire, 18" length

9 white buttons, ¼" diameter, for berries

Template material

White craft glue

making the ornament

1 Make a template of the mistletoe leaf pattern below and use it to cut a total of 12 leaves from the green wools.

2 Tie one leaf in a knot around the bottom of the wire. Wrap the wire around the knot to secure the leaf. Tie the remaining leaves in a knot along the length of wire so they stack on top of each other.

3 Bend the opposite end of the wire into a loop with the end against the top leaf; twist the wire together to secure.

FINISHED ORNAMENT
approximately 4" × 8" (including wire hanger)

4 Tie the red strip in a bow at the bottom of the hanging loop. Refer to the photo to glue the buttons to the leaves.

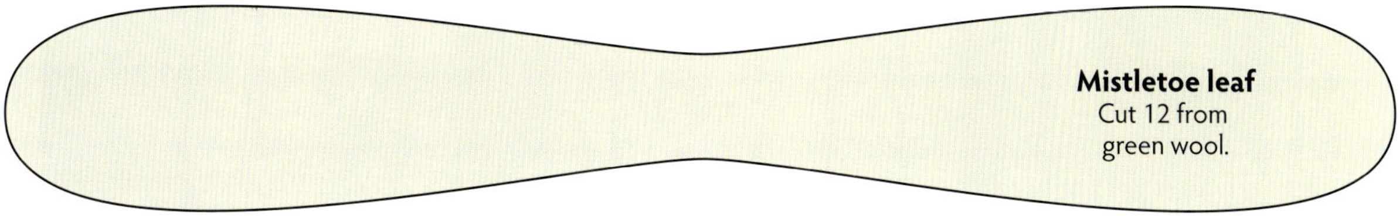

christmas candle mat

Turn your scraps into a whimsical mat that's perfect for tucking into a little holiday vignette in your home.

materials

Yardage is based on 42"-wide fabric. Fat quarters are 18" × 21".

Scraps of 6 assorted red prints for block

Scraps of 7 assorted green prints for block

1 fat quarter of tan Christmas print for appliqué background

3" × 3½" rectangle of green felted wool for tree branches

1" × 8" strip of brown felted wool for tree trunk

3½" × 7" rectangle of off-white felted wool for snowman

Scrap of orange felted wool for snowman nose

¼ yard of red print for binding

1 fat quarter of fabric for backing

14" × 17" piece of batting

Lightweight paper-backed fusible web

6-strand embroidery floss in colors to match wools

Size 7 embroidery needle

1 black button, ⅜" diameter, for chest

1 black button, ½" diameter, for belly

1 red button, ⅝" diameter, for treetop

cutting

All measurements include ¼"-wide seam allowances.

From the assorted green prints, cut a *total* of:

- 1 square, 2¾" × 2¾" (A)
- 1 rectangle, 1⅝" × 3⅞" (C)
- 1 rectangle, 1⅝" × 3⅞" (D)
- 1 rectangle, 1⅝" × 6⅛" (G)
- 1 rectangle, 1⅝" × 6⅛" (H)
- 1 rectangle, 1⅝" × 8⅜" (K)
- 1 rectangle, 1⅝" × 8⅜" (L)

From the assorted red prints, cut a *total* of:

- 1 rectangle, 1⅝" × 2¾" (B)
- 1 rectangle, 1⅝" × 5" (E)
- 1 rectangle, 1⅝" × 5" (F)
- 1 rectangle, 1⅝" × 7¼" (I)
- 1 rectangle, 1⅝" × 7¼" (J)
- 1 rectangle, 1⅝" × 9½" (M)

From the tan Christmas print, cut:

- 1 strip, 1½" × 13"
- 1 strip, 4" × 9½"

From the red print for binding, cut:

- 2 strips, 2½" × 42"

FINISHED CANDLE MAT
13" × 10½"

FINISHED BLOCK
9" × 9"

assembling the mat top

Use a ¼" seam allowance. Press the seam allowances as indicated by the arrows.

1 Sew a B rectangle to the right edge of an A square. Press. Add a C rectangle to the bottom edge of the unit. Press. Then add a D rectangle to the left and an E rectangle to the top of the unit to complete the first round, which should measure 5" square.

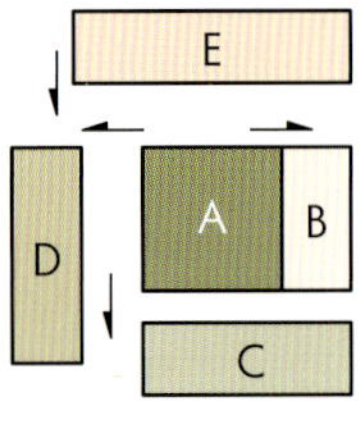

2 Working in a clockwise direction, continue adding rectangles F–M to the unit in alphabetical order to complete three rounds. The Log Cabin block should measure 9½" square, including seam allowances.

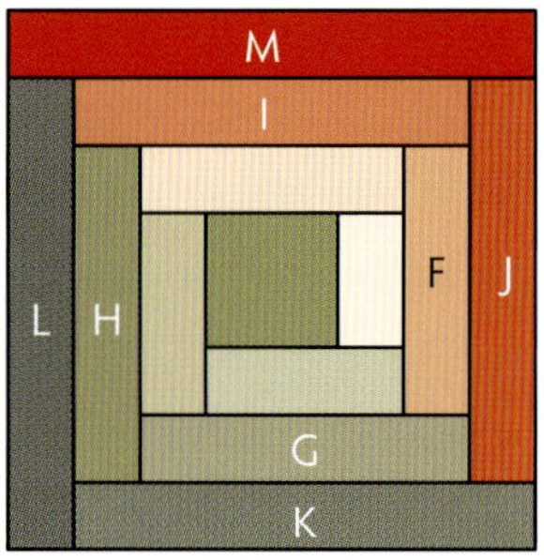

Make 1 block, 9½" × 9½".

3 Sew the tan 4" × 9½" strip to the left edge of the block. Press. Sew the tan 1½" × 13" strip to the bottom of the unit. Press. The mat top should measure 13" × 10½", including seam allowances.

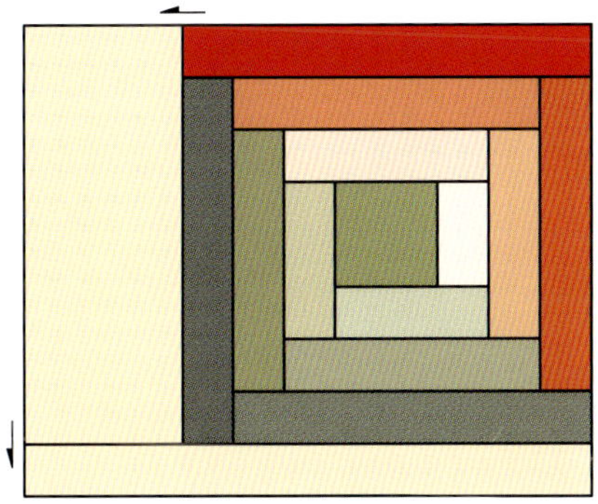

Candle-mat top,
13" × 10½"

finishing the mat

If you need detailed instructions about any of the finishing steps, download free information at ShopMartingale.com/HowtoQuilt.

1 Layer the backing, batting, and candle-mat top. Baste the layers together.

2 Quilt by hand or machine. The mat shown is quilted in the ditch of the seams.

3 Using the red 2½"-wide strips, make the binding and attach it to the mat.

4 Using the patterns on pullout pattern sheet 1 and referring to "Fusible-Web Appliqué" on page 78, prepare the appliqués. For the tree trunk, cut a 1" × 8" piece of fusible web and fuse it to the wrong side of the brown wool. From the prepared strip, cut one strip, ¼" × 5¾". For the tree branches, cut a 3" × 3½" rectangle of fusible web and fuse it to the wrong side of the green wool. From the prepared rectangle, cut ¼"-wide strips in each of the following lengths for the tree branches: 1¾", 3", 2⅛", 2½", and 2¾".

5 Refer to the appliqué placement guide to fuse the appliqués in place, positioning the branches on the trunk from shortest to longest. Referring to "Embroidery Stitches" on page 79 and using two strands of embroidery floss, whipstitch the appliqués in place. Using six strands of embroidery floss, make French knots for the eyes. Sew the black buttons to the front of the snowman. Sew the red button to the top of the tree trunk.

Appliqué placement guide

fusible-web appliqué

I use this technique for all of my wool appliqué. Fusing the shapes in place makes it easier to stitch around them without the shapes moving, and it's much easier to make the stitches when the thread isn't getting caught on pins!

1 Using a pencil, trace the number of appliqué shapes indicated on the project patterns onto the paper side of the fusible web, leaving approximately ¼" between each one.

2 Roughly cut out the shapes outside the drawn lines.

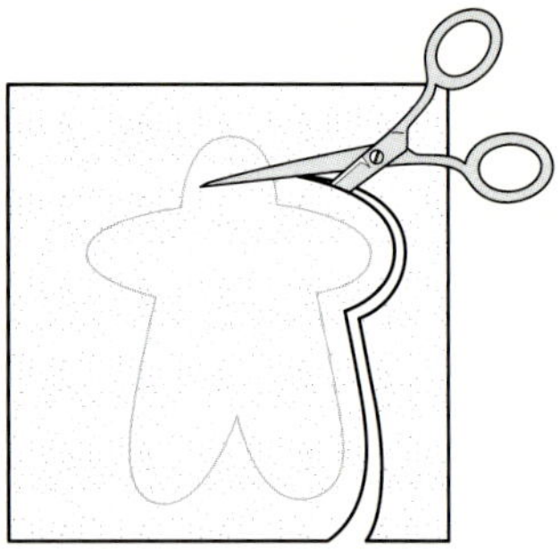

3 Follow the manufacturer's instructions to fuse each shape to the wrong side of the fabric indicated on the pattern.

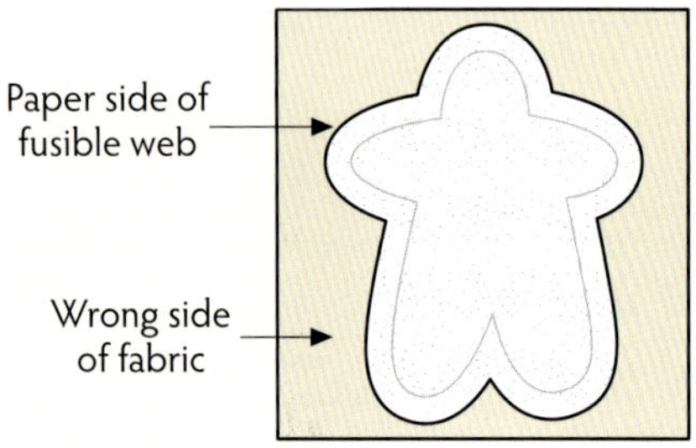

4 Cut out the shapes on the drawn lines.

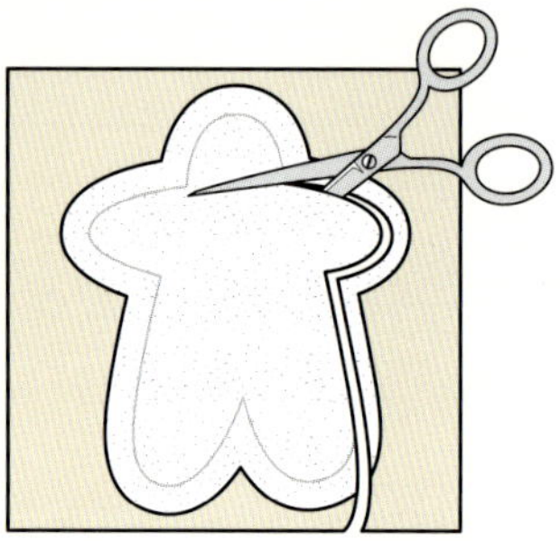

5 Remove the paper backing from each piece. Working on your ironing surface and referring to the project placement guide, arrange the shapes on the background piece. Fuse the shapes in place.

6 Using the stitch and thread indicated in the instructions and referring to "Embroidery Stitches" on page 79, stitch around each shape.

embroidery stitches

Embroidery is used to finish the edges of appliqués, as well as to add details. Unless otherwise indicated, use one strand of pearl cotton or two strands of embroidery floss to make the stitches.

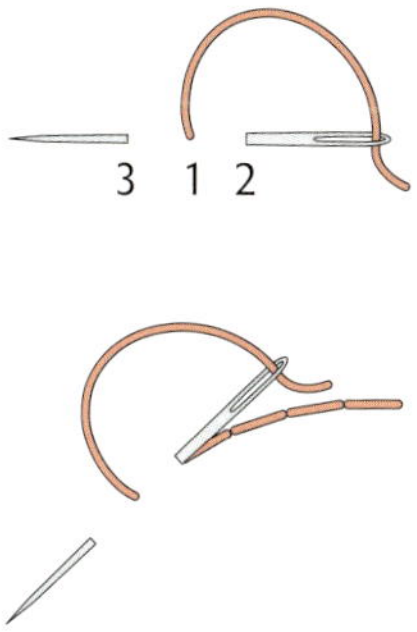

Backstitch

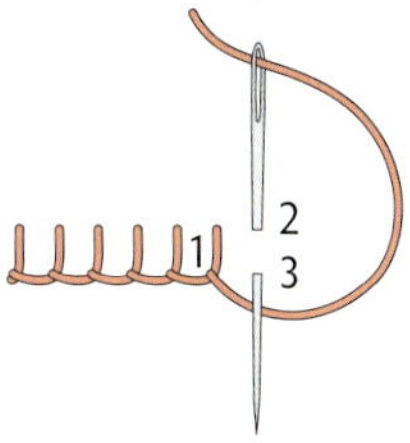

Blanket stitch

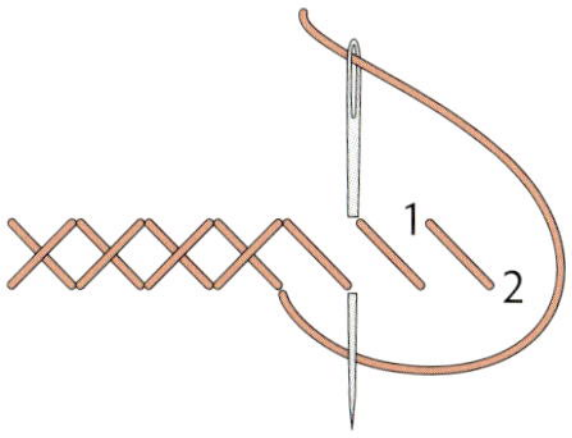

Cross-stitch

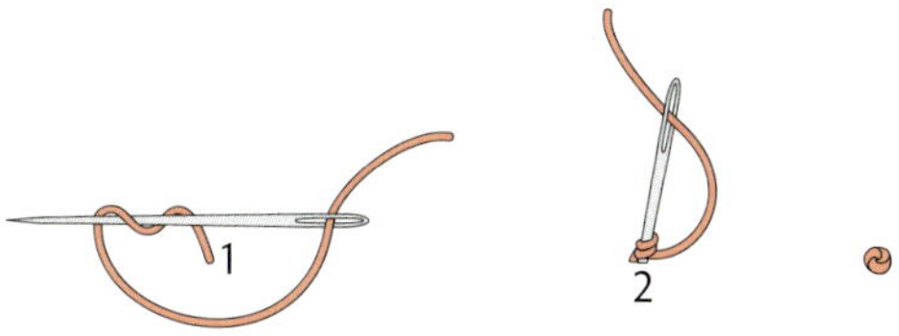

French knot

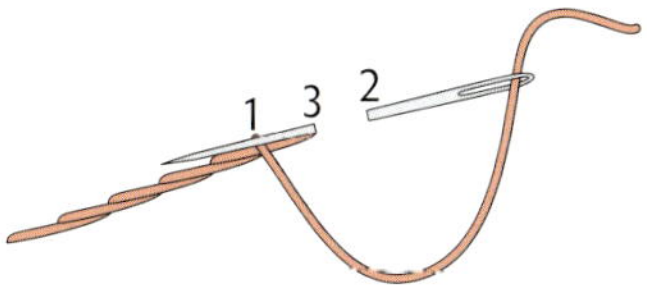

Stem stitch

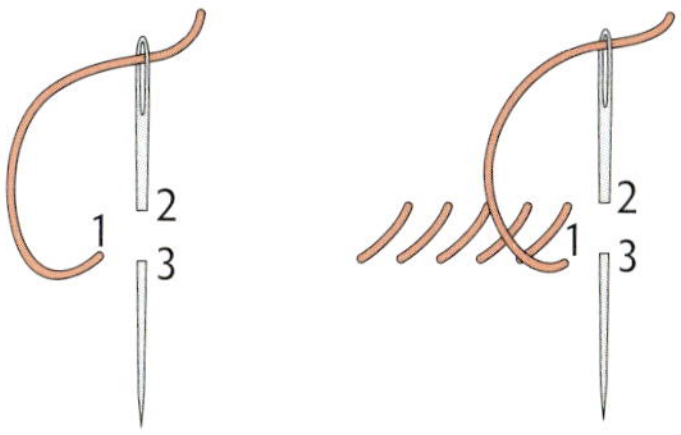

Whipstitch

about the author

A **longtime stitcher and quilt enthusiast,** Rhonda McCray started designing holiday quilt patterns in 2008, and that was the beginning of Farmhouse Threads. As the company expanded, family members were brought on board to help. Today Farmhouse Threads continues to be a family owned and operated venture based in Temecula, California.

Rhonda loves what she does, believing there's nothing more satisfying than providing quiltmakers with great patterns that contribute to the enjoyment, efficiency, and success of their quilting experience. Visit Rhonda at FarmhouseThreads.com.

HT 884375